swimming lessons
~ from ~
LUKAS

Learning to Live Beyond the Waves of Grief From My Infant's Death

NANCY HOVATTER

Swimming Lessons From Lukas
Copyright © 2018 by Nancy Hovatter

ISBN-10: 0-9990477-0-1
ISBN-13: 978-0-9990477-0-5

No part of this publication may be reproduced, stored in a retrieval system, or transmitted in any form or by any means, electronic, mechanical, photocopying, recording, or otherwise without written permission of the Publisher.

For information regarding permission, write to:
The Zebra Ink
publisher@thezebraink.com
The Zebra Ink, 410 Simpson Road,
Rochester, NY 14617
www.thezebraink.com

Printed in the United States of America
Copyeditor: Darcia Kunkel
Cover Design: Michelle Radomski
Interior Formatting: OneVoiceCan.com

To my children

Lukas, Jessica and Brenna ~

The wind beneath my wings

*"Grief is like the ocean.
It comes on waves ebbing and flowing.
Sometimes the water is calm.
Sometimes it is overwhelming.
All we can do is learn to swim."*

~ VICKI HARRISON ~

Acknowledgements

This book has been many years in the making with plenty of fits and starts. Although I knew I had a story within me, and one of my childhood dreams has always been to be a "writer," I never could find the confidence to write beyond the same four or five pages over and over again. I started other books with other topics, but I always came back to my story about Lukas, my grief, and how far I had come from that first terrible year after Lukas died. That was a pivotal moment in my life, and how I became the person I am today. My working title had always been "Becoming Nancy."

In the summer of 2015, I went to a friend's networking lunch and was inspired by the speaker. Her topic was: Five ways we sabotage ourselves to prevent our success. One of those five items sent bells and whistles off in my head because that is exactly what I was doing. I told her about my desire to write a book and why I "couldn't." I asked her about a coach. She said she knew someone who would be able to help me, and that is how I met Tricia Gibbons Reynolds.

After speaking with Tricia, I knew she was exactly what I needed to move me to write the book. I hired her to be my coach and mentor; to "hold my hand"; and hopefully get me out of my own way so I could embark on this path of being an author. Professionally, she is a coach and mentor with a Master of Arts in Spiritual Psychology. I learned she has various approaches to psychological development with an emphasis in spiritual counseling and effective interpersonal skills. She used all of them to get me to where you are reading my book today. Her passion is assisting clients who are at a crossroads in finding their unique voice, and then reflecting to them their innate strengths and Divine worth. She helps you "unblock" anything that keeps you from going after your creative projects and your lifelong dreams, while encouraging you to have presence and purpose in all that you do. At times, she was part coach, part mentor and part therapist. She was also my "editor"—reading my book as it was being written and offering her comments and suggestions. If it weren't for her, I would still be writing those same four or five pages. I am eternally grateful to you Tricia and will hold space and love for you forever in my heart.

Special thanks go to Sheila Kennedy: publisher, marketer and friend extraordinaire. From our first conversation, you inspired me with your positive outlook, confidence, fearlessness and expertise. My dream has always been to be an author. You have made that dream come true. Saying thank you seems inadequate.

Michelle Radomski created and designed the front and back covers and formatted the book. You have done a beautiful job, and it has been my privilege to work with you.

A huge thank you to Janet Kunst, my social media person, who designed and maintains my website. Janet also designed my Grief Coach Facebook page. The patience and education you have shown me for everything social media is herculean and deeply appreciated, especially through my endless questions and never-ending learning curve. If it weren't for you, I would have no social media presence.

To Dr. Janet Woods, I am so grateful I walked into the networking meeting you were hosting and for our friendship that developed from it. You were one of the first people to give me confidence and motivation; that whatever I wanted to do was doable and possible. I will be forever indebted to you for your question, "What would happen if you didn't think like that?" The first time you asked me that I was stunned into silence, because I had no answer for that question. I had never thought there was any other way to think. You forced me to think of possibilities and options, and thankfully I learned that anything is possible.

To my friend Joyce McBroom, I have nothing but love for you. I wrote the book while living in your home. You gave me the freedom to write, and when I came up for air, you were always eager to hear what I was writing. You were my sounding board. Your excitement about the book and assurance that the readers are out there gives me confidence.

To my brother and sister-in-law Marc and Jean Schwartz, my love, appreciation and gratitude for the two of you are endless. You both have supported and loved me unconditionally throughout my life. You have been there for me through the worst of times (more than once), and you have celebrated my happiness and success with love and joy. I am so happy to have both of you in my life.

And finally, to my children Lukas, Jessica and Brenna: it has been my greatest honor and privilege to be your mother. I love you all so much ... as we now say, "to the moon and back." Lukas, you will always be my sweet baby boy. Our life together is not what I planned or hoped for. I survived your death and learned how to thrive—something I didn't think possible. You are a part of me and always present in my life. Jessica and Brenna, you are the light of my life. You have brought me unimaginable joy. You gave me the best job in the world, and that is being your mom. All three of you taught me so much about myself that I did in fact "Become Nancy."

Table of Contents

Acknowledgements v

Introduction xi

Part I: Tsunami of Grief 1

Part II: Sharing the Life Preserver 65

Part III: Riding the Waves of Grief 83

Nancy Nuggets 113

Unwelcome and Unwanted Things
Said While Grieving 119

Swimming Lessons:
What to Say or Do for the Bereaved Parent 123

Letters to Lukas 127

About the Author 139

Introduction

I have always loved the beach. It is my happy place. I grew up in Brooklyn, NY, and for the first ten years of my life, my parents owned what would be called a "summer rooming house" at the end of Queens, NY. We lived there from Memorial Day in May until Labor Day in September. Families would take rooms for the summer. With no air conditioning at that time, it was always cooler at the beach. Our house was about 100 feet from the beach, and I was on the sand or in the ocean for about 8–10 hours every day. I learned to swim in the ocean.

I always respected the ocean and its currents. Even walking in ankle deep waves, I could always feel the pull of the current and knew how far I could go out. On the days when the ocean was warm and calm, I could just float for hours. I learned how to body surf before it was a "thing." Even today, give me a book, a beach chair, an umbrella and I'm happy.

Then the ocean showed me what it feels like to drown. When my son Lukas died, I was hit with one 50-foot emotional wave after another. My lungs were not filled with water, but with such deep sorrow and pain that it was all I could do to take a breath before another wave hit. Sometimes I thought it would be so much easier to drown. My pain would be over, and that was all that I wanted (besides of course my son). No one in my inner circle of family or friends had ever experienced what my then husband and I were going through. It seemed like they, too, were watching me drown. About 6 weeks after Lukas died, I was in a terrible car accident, which I was lucky to walk away from without a scratch. At the exact moment, I got out of my totaled car, and I knew I didn't want to drown. I wanted to live, and it would be up to me to save my own life. I was going to have to learn to swim through the 50-foot waves and be my own life-saver.

Just like I used to dive into huge oncoming waves and ride them to the shore, I allowed the waves of grief to engulf me. Honestly, I had no other choice. I couldn't just snap out of my emotions. I was swimming to keep my head above water and it wasn't always successful.

In writing this book 36+ years after Lukas' death, I can see all the swimming lessons I learned during my grief. While I was grief-stricken, I didn't realize I was learning anything other than my son died, and it was the worst time of my life.

Some of the swimming lessons I learned:

- There are no right or wrong ways to grieve.
- Couples grieve differently.
- There are no right or wrong emotions.
- Milestones, anniversaries, holidays can still set off 50-foot waves no matter how long ago.
- It's ok to ask for help.
- It's ok to change your mind.
- It's ok to laugh.
- You can rebuild your life and thrive.
- Your experience with your loss will impact you in ways you can't possibly imagine now.

During the in-between years, I had some serious medical issues, loss of jobs, and loss of a marriage. Each situation came with a new set of 50-foot waves. The difference each time was that I thought I've been here before; I am not going to drown, but the wave will be very rough for however long, until I can swim to shore.

PART I

Tsunami of Grief

In 1980 I was married and turning 30. My one goal was to have a baby (or at least be pregnant) by the time my birthday came around in December. My husband and I had been married three years, and just bought our first home. In today's terms, I had crossed off two items from my bucket list. The baby was next on the list.

I was thrilled to find myself pregnant in early 1980, and my baby was due September 20th —just about three months before my BIG 30. My excitement was tempered with some concern because in the beginning of my pregnancy I had a very bad cold and was taking lots of aspirin almost every four hours for several days. I don't remember if Tylenol was even around then as an alternative. Also, remember there was no Google to research this, so I couldn't find out if this could cause a problem to the baby. Technology wise, we were in the dark ages! When I went for my first OB appointment, I spoke to him about my fear about the aspirin and the possible effects on my baby. He was very reassuring that there would be no negative effect at all. There were three physicians in the group, and when I saw the other two for the first time, I was again reassured by each of them everything would be fine.

I put my concern in the back of my head, but it was still there. I read the baby books, and there was always a mention about drugs and pregnancy, even aspirin, but never anything conclusive or very negative. I did the best I could and relaxed. Hearing my baby's heartbeat for the first time was such a thrill, and I remember the doctor telling me what a strong heartbeat my baby had.

We started working on the nursery and getting our house ready. We put deposits on baby furniture and whatever else we needed. My extended family is neurotically superstitious, and I bought into their belief of not bringing anything for the baby into the house until you bring the baby into it, just in case "something happens." Being Jewish, we have a strong streak of neuroses/superstitions about not tempting the evil eye; who knows, but we had nothing in the house, and I certainly had no baby shower.

We took our Lamaze and baby prep classes. We toured the labor and delivery floor and the nursery. We practiced my breathing, so I could labor and deliver without drugs. My main reason for going "natural" was my fear of the epidural. As I said, my family history is filled with tales of neurotic horror and fear of what could possibly go wrong, so I was afraid I would be paralyzed forever if I took the epidural.

Three days before my due date, my water broke. We were thrilled. We called our family to let them know so they can be excited too and to prepare them for the change in all our lives.

We arrived at the hospital a little after midnight on September 17, 1980, ready to begin the biggest adventure of our lives so far. I was put into a cold, sterile labor room that didn't even have a chair, so my husband could have a seat. Thankfully those labor rooms don't exist anymore.

At 6 p.m. that night, I wasn't any further along in my labor than at midnight when I first arrived. I was given oral Pitocin to move my labor along and in one hour I dilated from 2cm to 10cm. From

7–9 p.m. I was in active labor and pushed for two hours to deliver the baby. I broke every blood vessel in my face but still no baby. So here comes the Epidural for the C-section. My Lamaze instructor had predicted that one of the couples in the class would need a C-section. I was the winner!

I was given the Epidural and was numb from under my breast to the bottom of my toes. I could wiggle my toes, and that is what I did throughout the entire C-section. With my husband sitting at my head, he asked the doctor if I was wiggling my toes because he knew about my fear. In my neurotic head, I just knew that if I could wiggle my toes, I would not be permanently paralyzed.

At 9:20 p.m. on September 17, 1980, Lukas T. arrived into this world. He weighed 9 lbs. and 5 oz. and was 21 inches long with a full head of black hair. In the Eastern European tradition of the Jewish religion, it is a common practice to name a baby after a family member who died. Per the *Jewish Book of Why*, to name a person after someone who is alive would rob that person of his full life if another member of the family were to carry his name in his lifetime. He was named after my mother Leonora (who had died six years earlier) and my husband's aunt Tillie (who had died long before that). We couldn't agree on a T name, so Lukas was given the middle initial T. My husband thought it sounded cool, and I didn't feel too strongly one way or the other about the T. I wanted my first baby to be named after my mother, and Lukas was. Was he beautiful? Of course! Was he the most beautiful of any baby in the entire world? Of course! I was strapped to the table being sewn up, so I didn't get to hold him, but I figured I would have a lifetime of holding him, so what did it matter? My husband said he was gorgeous and looked just like him! I let him have that moment!

After being in the recovery room, I was wheeled into my room about 10 p.m. I was completely exhausted from the long and difficult labor. I was given morphine for the pain when my epidural wore off, and I was becoming very sleepy. At that moment, I was not only feeling no pain, but still couldn't feel my body below my breasts to my toes. I knew the best thing for me was to go to sleep, so my neuroses could go to sleep as well. My husband left and said he would be back early in the morning.

Around midnight, the nurse woke me up and told me that my husband was coming back to the hospital. I looked at her and asked her if my baby died. She was stunned at the question and asked me why I would ask that. I replied, "Why would my husband come back two hours after he left if my son hadn't died? He was coming to tell me." She then told me that my son was having some "breathing problems," and the transport team from the hospital that had a higher level of care (an intensive care nursery) had been called and was coming to pick up Lukas.

My husband, Lukas, and the transport team arrived almost simultaneously to my room. He looked as stunned as I know I looked. The transport team started explaining what they thought was wrong with Lukas, and why they had been called. All I heard was blah, blah, blah—it was the aspirin that was causing these problems!

Their original diagnosis was that he had stenosis of the aorta, or his aorta was too small. Lukas' isolette was wheeled next to my bed so I could look at him. I put my finger through the opening of the isolette and he grabbed on. No one thought to take him out of the isolette, so I could hold him. I was too doped up to even request it. Smart phones were not invented yet, and no one had a traditional camera, so no photos were taken. I said my goodbye to my sweet baby boy, and he was wheeled out of my room. I never saw him again.

The next day, Thursday, was a blur. My husband spent a good part of the day at the hospital with Lukas, which was about ten miles away from me. He would call me periodically with updates, but there wasn't any good news. More tests, but inconclusive results. As the day dragged on, it became apparent that Lukas was a lot sicker than the original diagnosis, and that the intensive care nursery was not equipped to take care of him either. He needed to be transferred, yet again, to another hospital with the highest level of care for really sick babies/children. He was transferred to Children's Hospital of Philadelphia. We were in New Jersey, about two hours away.

My brother went with my husband. All my life, my older brother has been there for me, and continues to be an anchor for me to this day. My husband called me late Thursday night to tell me that Lukas was going to have heart surgery sometime on Friday. Although the doctors weren't certain what Lukas' problem was, they knew that it wasn't his aorta but his heart, and it was serious.

Meanwhile, I remained on the maternity floor in New Jersey. I shared a room with a new mom, her congratulatory balloons, flowers, excited family, and of course … her newborn baby. Today, most hospitals have private rooms for expectant moms. The labor, deliver and recovery are all in one room. In 1980, that concept hadn't been invented yet.

So, the wait began. The only person who gave me any kind of hope was a nurse on the Thursday night shift. She had had triplets, and they, too, were transferred to Children's Hospital of Philadelphia (CHOP) and were now thriving six months later. She told me what a fantastic hospital it was, and that my son was in perfect hands. I held on to her confidence.

Friday, my husband and my brother were back at CHOP awaiting the latest test results. My husband called me around noon to tell me that whatever Lukas had was definitely a defect with his heart, and he was being prepped for open-heart surgery. He later told me that the doctors thought they had a diagnosis of Hypoplastic Left Heart Syndrome but wouldn't know for sure until they saw Lukas' heart. He couldn't really tell me what it was, other than his heart was "not right."

I later learned that Hypoplastic Left Heart Syndrome (HPLHS) is a severe congenital heart defect in which the left side of the heart is critically underdeveloped. The heart's left side has the job of pumping oxygenated blood into the aorta, the larger artery that carries blood to the body. If a baby is born with HPLHS, the left side of the heart cannot efficiently pump blood to the body, so the right side of the heart must pump blood both to the lungs and to the rest of the body. It is too much of a stress to require the right side to do this, and eventually it cannot continue to pump blood to both places. In a very short amount of time, the right ventricle is too weak to continue, stops functioning and the baby dies. The National Birth Defects Prevention Network estimates that birth defects occur in about three percent of live births in the US. Of this, HPLHS occurs in one of 4,344 live births, or an estimated total of 960 live births every year in the US.

Dr. William Norwood, a cardiologist at Children's Hospital of Boston, had developed a new procedure for HPLHS patients. A new aorta is built, turning part of the baby's pulmonary artery (the one that normally goes from the heart to the lungs) into a "new aorta." The right ventricle would pump blood to the body through the new aorta. This would create a passage between the new aorta and the original pulmonary artery, and some blood would get to the lungs. He first developed this procedure in 1979, and it was becoming the standard protocol of care for HPLHS babies. To this day, this is the first step in treating HPLHS babies. It is, in fact, called the Norwood Procedure. If the patient lived through this first surgery (which at the time had a very low survival rate), the baby would need two more surgeries over the next two years with high mortality rate for each surgery. Because the procedure was so new, very little data was available about the future physical and neurological outcomes of these babies.

Lukas was taken to surgery on Friday, September 19 around 10 a.m., and somewhere around noon my husband called me to tell me that he didn't make it. Lukas had died on the operating table. I remember throwing the phone down and screaming, "It was the aspirins. I killed my baby with those aspirins!" My father and his wife were up from Florida and in my room when my husband called. Shocked and stunned silence filled the room. I remember looking at the congratulatory flowers in my room and screaming to have those flowers taken out. Then nothing. My husband and my brother arrived about two hours later, and everyone filed out to give us some private time. My husband sat in the chair next to my bed, and I was in my bed. We just stared at each other and said nothing. We couldn't comfort each other because we were hurting so badly. When I look back at it now, I see that was the way each of us would grieve … separately and alone.

Today, most hospitals have a protocol for a fetal demise or a still-birth. The parents are given a lock of their baby's hair, the swaddling blanket he was wrapped in, a copy of his footprints, his wristband, and photos that were taken if the baby was stillborn. All of this is given to the Perinatal Social Worker and then offered to the parents. If the baby is born alive, a birth certificate is issued.

———————————SWIMMING LESSONS———————————

You may claim your child as a dependent on that year's taxes, as the baby was alive even if only one breath was taken. This is a way to validate the baby's existence.

The parents are told that if they don't want their "memory box" right now, the Social Work Department will keep it until they decide they do. There is also some sort of marker (a flower or a leaf) placed on the door to the mom's room and on her chart to let the staff know that her baby has died. The social worker also comes to speak with the parents to tell them of the bereavement resources available either at the hospital or in the community. The hospital chaplain or the parents' religious representative may be called as well. In 1980, these protocols were not yet in place, and nothing was offered to me. I was totally alone.

Many cemeteries have a "baby" or "angel" section. A public ceremony, like a funeral, validates the baby's existence and acknowledges that this baby was real—not a blob of tissue, BUT a member of a family. A public ceremony is an acknowledgement of that person regardless how long the baby lived, if at all. We didn't have a public ceremony. We didn't think of it, nor did anyone suggest it. My brother took care of all the arrangements, and he and my husband picked out the site where Lukas would go. The director of the cemetery encouraged my husband not to tell me where Lukas was buried because that would be better for me. He said to tell me that he is "over there somewhere". He knew that I would never stand for that, so he just ignored that bit of "advice."

Meanwhile, I was recovering from a C-section, and in those days, insurance companies allowed moms to recover in the hospital for as long as they needed. I had also developed an infection, and every 12 hours, I was given a massive injection of Penicillin. The dosage and needle were so great that I had to have a warm towel placed on the injection site afterwards, and then had to walk off the pain. I knew I deserved the pain. I had killed my baby. I never complained.

For the next ten days, due to the infection, I was in the hospital. I shared a room with two different new moms. I had been instructed to walk, so I would walk around the floor. I felt like I was the pariah of the floor. The nursing staff averted their eyes. You could almost feel the dread they felt when they had to come into my section of the room. On Sunday, two days after Lukas died, one of my doctors came in for daily rounds. This was the first time I had seen him since Lukas was born. Remember, there were three physicians in this practice. Doctor A delivered me and was on hospital duty until Friday.

Doctor B came to see me Friday night and Saturday, and now Doctor C was in my room.

Dr. C and the nurse came in to my room for his daily rounds, and by then my milk had come in. What a cruel joke "Mother" Nature plays on a mom of a dead baby. Our body doesn't know that our baby died, and we have no one to nurture. I asked him if he could give me something to dry up my milk. He looked at me strangely and said, "I thought you were breastfeeding your baby." You know the expression "it was so quiet you could hear a pin drop?" This was that moment. The nurse turned green and looked pensively from me to the doctor. I looked at him and said, "Yes, I would love to breastfeed my baby, but he died, and if you can show me how to breastfeed him, I would love it." Then I screamed, "Don't you know my baby died? Get out of my room and don't ever come back!" It is 36+ years later, and I can recall it like it was yesterday. Awkward conversations like that are avoided today because protocols are in place to indicate on the door or chart that a baby has passed.

The rest of my stay in the hospital was really more of the same. As for my husband, he went to the stores to collect our deposits. Even without bringing anything into our house, "something happened." Another lottery we didn't want to win. He came to the hospital every day. He answered every question I had about Lukas' time in both hospitals. I asked him the same questions over and over, with him giving me the same answers time and time again. I think this was a combination of me not being able to remember information, and me wanting/needing to hear every detail so at least, vicariously, I was with Lukas.

I couldn't wait to leave the hospital but was terrified to leave the hospital. While there, I was sort of in a cocoon where I could somehow fool myself into not thinking of anything but staying in bed and walking when I had to. Finally, after 12 days of my hospital stay, I was discharged. This, too, was another reminder of how I was going home empty handed. I was put in a wheelchair and taken to the elevator by a nurse while my husband went to get the car. When the nurse and I were waiting for the elevator, another mother holding her newborn son wrapped in a blue blanket (and her nurse holding the flowers and balloons) was also waiting for the elevator. We got into it together; rode down to the lobby; and were wheeled outside together while we waited for our cars. She was filled with excitement, and I was filled with loss.

We drove home in silence. What was there to say? This was not the homecoming I had planned or envisioned. I imagined coming home to a house filled with flowers, banners, and streamers welcoming Lukas and I home. His bedroom would be all set up with all the furniture finally delivered, and all the clothes that my mother-in-law was storing for us folded in his dresser and hanging in the closet. Instead, my husband and I walked into our home that was filled with silence and death.

Sadie, our dog, was anxiously waiting to greet me, and was so excited to see me after 12 days of being away. Her tail was wagging, and she was jumping in place—ready to pounce on me if I gave the signal. Instead, very solemnly I greeted her and began to cry. She seemed to know intuitively that something was wrong and just stopped. She was waiting for me, and I didn't know what to do. I sat in a chair, and she came to my side and just sat there with her head in my lap. As I began to cry, she slowly licked my hand. Years later, I would think of that gesture as something a mother does when her child gets hurt. "Come, let mommy kiss your boo-boo and make it all better." If only she could.

Looking back now after 36+ years, I can't really tell you how I spent each day those first few weeks. I know that I wasn't sleeping that much or well, or eating, or even talking. My husband went to work each day and I didn't. I just sat with Sadie lovingly at my side. I didn't answer the phone. In 1980, we didn't have answering machines yet, so people had to wait to speak to me when my husband got home (and only then if I was able or wanted to speak). I later designed a system for the people I wanted to speak with: "Call and let the phone ring three times, hang up and then call back. Then I will speak with you."

Getting the mail was just another reminder of our dead son. Mixed in with sympathy cards were congratulatory cards of little boys and balloons, as well as coupons for baby food, diapers, and baby's first professional photo.

I was recovering from surgery, so I was still in lots of pain. I would caress my C-section scar because that was where Lukas came from. It somehow kept me connected to him. Each day seemed so much longer than 24 hours. All I could do to fill my hours was cry and realize that I had no baby. As slow as each day felt, it was taking me further and further away from him. I was so afraid of losing him to time in the distance.

Every day was the same. I would have about ten seconds of peace when I opened my eyes and "forget" that Lukas wasn't here, but then reality would set in. There were times I thought for sure I was crazy because I swore I would hear him crying. I really couldn't function. I had no concentration and couldn't follow even the most basic of things, such as TV shows or even TV commercials. I absolutely couldn't read … not even magazines or newspapers.

My car became a sanctuary for me, because I cried unabashedly from the moment I turned on the ignition to the time I turned it off. I never seemed to wind up where I was supposed to go, such as the grocery store. I seemed to get on the road and drive. Sooner or later, I would realize that I was someplace, but I didn't know how I got there and would turn around and head home. If I made it to the grocery store, all I seemed to see were pregnant women, newborns, or toddlers, and this was so painful for me. I soon learned the best thing was to just stay home and live each miserable second without my baby until it was time to go to bed; then to start the same day over again. I was living Groundhog Day before the movie had even been written!

I went for my six-week checkup, which, again, was a nightmare for me. There I was in the waiting room … with moms, their newborns, and very pregnant women. They were so happy, and I couldn't look at them. My doctor did ask me how I was doing, but that was really the extent of any kind of support. We didn't even discuss Lukas' diagnosis. All he said was that after two periods I could try to get pregnant again.

Waiting two months is the standard medical advice given to women who have suffered a loss. The assumption is that it takes two months for your body to recover from the pregnancy; However, there is no mention of how long it takes to recover from the emotional trauma. What I have learned in my years of working with the grief stricken, is that time is measured in two ways. The first is chronological: hours, days, weeks, months, and years. The other measurement is personal: how long it takes for a person to process the experience. Each individual goes through this process uniquely, and it will take as long as it takes. After two months, I was nowhere near ready to think about getting pregnant again. I needed my time with Lukas and my grief. This was our time together, and I wasn't able or ready to give it up.

Family and friends did the best they could, but they couldn't understand what I was going through. There was no one in our circle who had ever had this kind of loss. Hearing that I was young and could have other children was NOT what I wanted to hear and was definitely NOT comforting. The next bit of advice I got was to keep busy and go back to work. I had quit my job to be a stay at home mother. Since that wasn't happening, maybe I should think about going back to work. After all, maybe my family knew what was best for me because I was so out of it, I couldn't think.

On Election Day in 1980, I went out on a job interview. This was about six weeks after Lukas died. I don't remember the job or the interview. All I remember was my drive home. It was pouring down rain. As I was getting off one road to merge onto another I hydroplaned. I was in the left lane of a six-lane highway (three lanes in both directions). From the left lane, I crossed the two other lanes, up the embankment, back down across the three lanes, over the median across the three lanes of oncoming traffic, and hit the guardrail. I didn't hit another car, and I walked out of my car without any injury.

I didn't realize it then, but I had two so called "epiphanies:"

- I didn't want to die. Although I never considered suicide, I didn't care if I were to die. I saw death as a way out of my pain. This accident made me realize that I did want to live—even with the loss of Lukas and the accompanying pain.
- The only reason I was in the car looking for a job was because I assumed other people knew what was best for me. That wasn't true then, and it isn't true for me now. If I had listened to my inner voice, I would have known I wasn't ready for a job. I didn't realize these thoughts at the time and I don't know when I incorporated them into my life, but I can tell you that 36+ years later, I have met many difficult challenges in my life with those two thoughts.

———————————SWIMMING LESSONS———————————

Learn to ignore advice that you know is not correct or helpful for you.

We were now in November, and I was being bombarded with reminders everywhere about the coming holidays. What no one tells you is that your first holiday season without your loved one is especially difficult. Everybody seems so happy and full-on into their traditions. For people who are grieving, the day of the holiday, the days leading up the holiday, or even the days after the holiday can be very difficult. We were not celebrating, as we didn't have anything to feel joyful about. The holidays were a reminder of who was not with us.

The celebrations and photos I imagined and dreamed of with Lukas were not the reality I was living. I had ignored Halloween completely, and did not answer the door. This was my favorite holiday, as I loved seeing the children dress up. Lukas was going to be a pumpkin. Thanksgiving was approaching. My husband was a very good cook and worked in the food industry. His favorite meal to prepare has always been Thanksgiving. I had imagined a photo with Lukas and the turkey drumstick in front of him. In the years before this Thanksgiving, we would have both families plus any person we knew who didn't have a place to go. That year we just had his parents. What I remember about that Thanksgiving was how quiet we were. There wasn't much talking … each of us in our thoughts of what was; what was supposed to be; and how it really was.

On December 8th, John Lennon was murdered. I know this might sound strange, but this really added to my grief. I was a huge Beatles fan, and John was my favorite. He gave me my first sexual inkling (although I didn't know what that was at the time). This peaceful, beautiful, and talented man had been killed in front of his wife for no reason. I felt a strange kinship with his wife Yoko Ono. She was suffering with an unimaginable loss the same way I was. The only difference was the entire world was mourning with her. John Lennon's death on top of my son's death was truly the death of my youth.

The following week was my 30th birthday. I was very explicit with my friends and family that I wanted absolutely no acknowledgement of my birthday. When you are a teenager or in your 20s, turning 30 is a huge emotional milestone. You are no longer a kid. You are a full-blown adult, and perhaps you are living your dreams (marriage, job, family, etc.). I was lost at sea; old beyond my years. Birthday celebrations would have to wait.

Two weeks later was Christmas. Although my husband and I are Jewish, his family always celebrated Christmas as a "seasonal" holiday, and my mother-in-law went crazy with buying gifts. She seemed to be shopping all year, and when the day finally arrived, you seemed to be opening presents for hours. She wrapped everything in a separate box, even if she bought six pairs of socks they were in six separate boxes. I knew this was going to be a challenge, and I just couldn't see myself participating, but I also knew how important this was to my husband. After much thought and discussion, we agreed that we would go to his mother's house for dinner. All the presents for everyone else had to have been opened with our gifts put in a shopping bag which we would open when we got home. We would not be giving any gifts.

SWIMMING LESSONS

Traditions can be changed, and you can even choose to ignore the holiday. Just because you celebrate a holiday or a family milestone a certain way every year, doesn't mean you can't change it when you need to.

The important thing is to figure out what will comfort you the most or cause you the least amount of pain. Be sure to communicate your feelings with your family. They don't have to like it or understand it but accept it because you are asking them to do it. For us, we didn't "celebrate" Christmas we "observed" it.

My husband and I grieved very differently from each other, and that I couldn't understand. We both experienced the same loss, yet we were worlds apart in our reactions. I cried all the time, and he seemed to never cry. I wanted to talk about Lukas and his hospital stay all the time; he didn't. He talked about the future and eventually having another baby. I still wanted Lukas. He went to work and functioned. I sat on the couch. I learned that this is very common with couples. One of the hardest things to do while grieving your loss is to respect and "allow" your partner to grieve their own way.

SWIMMING LESSONS

Having two parents grieve differently is not unusual.

Learning to accept how each of you grieves can be an additional challenge.

This became a real challenge for us. It became crystal clear about two months later when we were at the mall. When exiting the mall, we walked through the baby section of Sears, and by the time we got to the car, I was in tears. My husband took one look at me, asked me what was wrong. I couldn't believe he would even ask that question! So very naturally I said walking through the baby section just set me off. He just exploded and threw the packages all over the parking lot. He started screaming at me that he couldn't take my tears anymore and he was "done." So now, not only did I lose my baby, it looked like I was going lose my husband and marriage.

A few days later I called the neonatologist who had taken care of Lukas. I started to cry to him that I was still so grief stricken, and now I thought my husband and I were going to split up. He told me that what I was experiencing was "normal" grief reactions, and that it wasn't unusual for couples to grieve differently. He offered to see us to review Lukas' diagnosis, answer any questions we had, and to talk about grief. I gladly made an appointment, and when my husband got home later that day, told him we were going to see Dr. H.

Seeing Dr. H was wonderful. The first thing he told us was that Lukas' HPLHS, unfortunately, is "just one of those things" that occurs. It is a birth defect. It had ABSOLUTELY NOTHING to do with my taking aspirins—nothing caused it, and nothing can prevent it from happening. He talked about grief and how it is usual, rather than unusual, for couples to grieve differently. Specifically, men are socialized to be the stoic protector and fixer in the family. Well, in our case, nothing could fix Lukas. My husband couldn't take my pain away as much as Sadie tried to do every day. Dr. H also said that women usually feel responsible, thinking that it was something we did or didn't do to cause our baby to die. Boy, did he hit the nail on the head with that.

We talked about another pregnancy. I told him that my husband was ready, and I clearly wasn't. Again, typical. I did ask him about HPLHS happening again or even testing for it, and he said there was no test for it. Yes, it could happen again, but we were only at a slightly higher risk for any kind of cardiology problem than other couples because of Lukas. We would have to take our chances with another pregnancy. I knew at that moment that I would have to be so much stronger. I would have to want another baby so much that I was willing to experience another loss again.

———————————SWIMMING LESSONS———————————

Make an appointment to speak with your doctor specifically to answer your questions about your pregnancy and loss. Write them out beforehand, and then write in the answers. The session with your doctor may be reassuring in lessening any guilt you feel about what you may or may not have done to cause your baby to die.

In early 1981, a book called *When Pregnancy Fails* was published by two mothers whose babies had died. This book was their story, but it was also a story for all other mothers/fathers whose babies had died. It was a source of comfort for me. For the first time since Lukas had died, I was reading words and thoughts that could have very easily come out of my mouth. I wasn't alone anymore. These two women knew what I was going through because they had lived it. I remember sitting on my couch and reading this book from cover to cover without stopping. Then I re-read it again with a yellow highlighter, underlining passages that resonated with me. It seemed the entire book was covered in yellow. This became my Bible. I read it every day. These women spoke my truth, and whenever I doubted what I was feeling, I picked up the book; re-read certain passages; and was validated. What I learned was that I was NORMAL. I wasn't crazy! I was grief-stricken, and although I didn't know it then, I was going through the stages of grief. If I ever wanted to feel good and happy again, I would have to live my grief—minute by miserable minute until I was able to resolve and accept the death of Lukas. I didn't know how long accepting Lukas' death would take, but knowing these women had accepted their children's deaths, gave me hope that I could do that too.

My cousin Barbara, who is two weeks younger than I am, also helped me. We are "sisters" without the sibling rivalry, and we had always been there for each other. When Lukas died, she was in nursing school getting her Nurse Practitioner degree. No matter what she was doing, she stopped so she could take my call. It was to her, I cried when I knew I couldn't do it with my husband. It was to her, I spoke of my continuing pain and the fear that I would never have another child. She told me about *When Pregnancy Fails*. Barbara just listened, never trying to "fix" what I was going through. I am grateful to her to this day.

I have always been able to express my feelings, and I love to write. I started writing letters, not knowing this would be very healing for me. I didn't know to whom I would write or what I would say, but I started writing letters. My first few letters were to Lukas apologizing to him, for not being able to "grow" him whole, and that I wasn't with him at both hospitals. I apologized for the aspirins, even though that wasn't what caused his HPLHS. I wrote about my pregnancy with him and how I felt about each milestone we achieved, like hearing his heart beat for the first time or feeling him move. I wrote about his delivery, and how I was so sorry I never got to hold him and coo over him like every new mother. I told him about the room that was waiting for him, and how his dad had painted, and wall papered his nursery. I also told him who his parents were; the life I planned for the three of us; and the siblings I hoped would come a few years later. Much later, I realized that through these letters, not only was I parenting him the only way I could, but I was also giving him and me a past, present and future—one that we would always have together. Ultimately, I also asked for his forgiveness … once I had forgiven myself.

I also wrote letters to other people. I found that so many of my friends fell into one of two groups: those that I had expectations of "being there for me" and those that I didn't expect much. I was disappointed and surprised when people who I thought would be in one group, turned out to be in the other. For those that disappointed and hurt me, I wrote scathing letters about how much I was hurt by them. I wasn't tactful; I was brutal. However, I never mailed them. I wrote what I needed to say to them and that was enough.

I don't know how I realized that it was important for me to get my feelings out, so I could finally let them go. Keeping them bottled up inside of me only made me hurt more. I needed to heal, and I knew I had to speak my truth. In the long run, I lost them as friends, not because of what I said to them (at least not aloud), but because I couldn't see their humanity in my experience. Unfortunately, this becomes another loss, and for some people, they cannot handle another loss; that is ok. Looking back over the years, I can honestly say that these losses were good for me. When I confronted one person and asked her why she never called me or sent a card, she said she didn't know what to say! I know that if she had known me when my mother had died, she would have said, "I'm sorry." That was the least I felt I deserved.

I also wrote letters to my husband saying to him what we could not discuss in person. I was ok with doing it this way because I was letting go of so much I needed to say, and knew it was too painful for him to hear. I never told him that I wrote them, nor did I ever give them to him. I didn't save them. They had served my purpose.

I also wrote myself letters of forgiveness. I didn't know it at the time, but these letters turned out to be one of the very last steps in helping me let go of my grief. By forgiving myself for everything that happened, whether it was in my control or not (HPLHS), I was finally accepting the reality of Lukas' death. The extreme pain I had experienced had abated, and I was finally able to think about him with love and perhaps "what could/should have been." I was ready to face the future, whatever that meant. I was still on somewhat shaky ground and wasn't ready to get pregnant again. I knew that was something that I would be thinking about—even though that thought terrified me. I knew that we would eventually try again. I wasn't crying all the time anymore. I was sleeping. I had renewed interest in life and was starting to go out with my husband and with friends. I still had my moments of extreme sadness, pain, and loss, but they were certainly more manageable and shorter in duration.

──────────────── SWIMMING LESSONS ────────────────

Find a way to release the feelings you are experiencing.

Writing/journaling works for me. Others create art, confide in a friend, or use yoga, meditation, etc. to show their pain. The purpose is to express your feelings so eventually you can let them go.

About six months later, I found a new job and met new people. As I said, I was still on shaky ground, so I didn't tell anyone about Lukas. I couldn't face their questions, pity, blame, or sorrow for me. It was very difficult at times because some of the women in the office were my age and getting pregnant. I was faced with their growing bellies and excitement. To make matters worse, some of them had children Lukas' age. Yes, those were tough times, and often I had to go into my car to cry, because at those moments the pain returned with a vengeance.

There are questions people ask (thinking that they are harmless) as a step to getting to know you like, "Do you have any children?" or "How many children do you have?" I realized the first time I was asked, that this would be a lifelong question I would have to answer and needed to adjust accordingly. If I said no, then I felt as if I betrayed my child, making it look like he never existed. If I said yes, then I would have to explain how and why my child died. I risked being faced with reliving my story and the pain. It really is a no-win situation.

────────── SWIMMING LESSONS ──────────

Answer questions about the existence of your child that died however you feel the most comfortable.

If you are never going to see this person again, the short answer can be no, even though you and your child know the truth. If you know this person will be in your life for a long time, then tell them the truth when you can. You don't have to go into a long explanation with all the details. You could just say, "My son/daughter had a birth defect and died shortly after birth." or "He/she was stillborn." or "I had a miscarriage." You can answer in such a way that no more questions will be forthcoming. This took me a long time to figure out. I just said no for the longest time (and felt tremendous guilt and sadness), but as time passed, I got stronger in telling the truth. I was able to say my son was born with a heart defect and lived two days. Interestingly, these complete strangers would say to me how sorry they were, and then we would move on.

I soon grew to love this job. It wasn't far from my house, and my boss was a nice man who reminded me of my Jewish grandfather. I didn't tell him or anyone else in the office about Lukas. It was still too fresh. I couldn't face the questions, or what I thought would be their judgments—that I had done something to contribute to my son's death. When people asked me about my past, I said that my husband and I were living in New York and bought our house in New Jersey in July. After a few months of commuting from New Jersey to New York for my job, I decided to take some time off and look for a job closer to my home. There was no reason for anyone to doubt me, and this became my story.

May was fast approaching, and so was my first Mother's Day. I felt like there is no greater torture than to have the world celebrate Mother's Day when you have a dead child. Was I still a mother if I had no living proof? Mine was in the cemetery. I knew this was going to be a tough day for me, and for my husband. He would be watching me go through the day, while also re-imagining how he thought we would have spent our first Mother's and Father's Day if Lukas had lived.

I decided to do something to acknowledge Lukas. In the Jewish tradition, there is a service of commemoration called an unveiling. It is a formal ceremony to dedicate the monument (headstone/footstone) that has been erected. A veil or cloth is draped over the stone, and the words inscribed on the stone are usually covered so that a member of the family will have the honor of "officially" unveiling it (the moment the inscription will be seen for the first time by the public). This would be the public acknowledgement of our son, since we did not have a funeral. This would be our chance to honor Lukas and to have him take his rightful place in our family.

A week before Mother's Day, we had a very small service with my brother, his family, and my in-laws plus a Rabbi attending. We had our unveiling. Before the service, I spoke with the Rabbi about certain things I wanted him to say, and he was very accommodating. At the service, he said how much Lukas was loved and wanted; how he would always be our first child and first grandchild for my husband's family; how he will always be a member of our family and remembered; and how we will carry him in our hearts forever. This service was so very healing for me. I knew I had turned a corner.

――――――――― SWIMMING LESSONS ―――――――――

My recommendation is to have a memorial service anytime you need or want to. Time or distance doesn't matter. Do it when it feels right for you.

Ugh! I still had to get through Mothers' Day the following week. It was a very difficult week leading up to the actual day. I went right back to feeling miserable and crying. I missed my Lukas so badly that my whole body ached. No one from my circle of family or friends contacted us all week. They knew we were suffering, and what could they say anyway? Mother's Day arrived, and I woke up with a tremendous headache, wanting to stay in bed all day. This wasn't possible. We had to face this day, just like we faced every other day without Lukas since the day he died. We decided to take a drive down to the Jersey Shore and have some lunch. I always feel so calm and serene at the ocean. We really didn't say much, but I was glad to get out of the house and to the beach. We were very much in our own thoughts, but I knew that at least for this day, we were thinking about the same thing. We were gone for most of the afternoon and stopped at the cemetery on our way home. I needed to be with my son. I needed to acknowledge that I was a mother. When we got home, inside our front door there were flowers waiting for me. The card just simply said, "Babe, Next Year."

The following month was Father's Day, and once again I felt bereft. It wasn't in my husband's nature to discuss his feelings, but I knew he was missing his son. He and his father had been estranged since his father walked out on him when he was 10 (ten) years old. He was now 32. He desperately wanted a child, and I knew how elated he was when Lukas was born because he would finally have a father-son connection. Again, we went for a ride down to the beach and had lunch outside. It was one of those glorious sunny Jersey summer days at the shore. So many families with children of all ages had the same idea, and there we were amongst them … observing, but not celebrating Father's Day, as our child wasn't with us. We managed to get through the day as we had gotten through every other day, whether it was memorialized as a holiday or not. Although we didn't discuss another child, alone in our thoughts I knew we were thinking that perhaps next year we would have proof that we were parents.

July was the month of our fifth wedding anniversary: another day to observe; another empty holiday; another day for me to remember what I had planned and what my reality was now. It's hard to remember back so many years ago, but I'm sure I got a card from my husband and definitely no gift. I know I told everyone in the family and in my circle of friends that I would have no celebrations of any kind until further notice, and that was honored. I do believe that keeping with our past tradition, we went to the shore for a nice quiet dinner.

The next big day(s) would be September 17th–19th—the time of Lukas' life and death. It also meant that our year of firsts—all the holidays, milestones, and traditions without our son—was ending. As much as I didn't think I would be able to, I had lived an entire year without my son. I realize now looking back, I needed every second of the entire year to grieve for my son. I needed to experience every single emotion on the spectrum. No one could "snap me out of it." I had to work on my grief, and through my grief to let go of my grief and come out the other side.

SWIMMING LESSONS

There is no timeline in grief. It is different for each person.

Many grief experts believe there are stages to grief. The pioneer of this philosophy is Elizabeth Kubler-Ross, M.D., a Swiss-born psychiatrist, and the author of the groundbreaking book *On Death and Dying* (1969). She first discussed what is now known as the Kubler-Ross model, in which she proposed the Five Stages of Grief as a pattern of adjustment. The five stages are **denial, anger, bargaining, depression and acceptance**. She stated that in general, individuals experience most of these stages (though in no defined sequence) after being faced with the reality of their own impending death. The five stages have since been adopted by many as applying to the survivors of a loved one's death as well. Did I experience the five stages? I would say yes, although I never "knew" of them as stages, nor did I know when I was moving in or out of them. Would it have helped me to know that I was experiencing these stages? **No. I couldn't come out of them until I was done experiencing them.**

As time passed and I resolved my feelings, I knew I was healing—even if it was incrementally. Time was a great healer for me, as was the unveiling. I also knew I was doing much better when I could think of future things—not necessarily another baby, but just something in the future, like planning to visit friends or a vacation. I knew I was in the stage of acceptance when on the night of September 17, 1981, my brother called me to ask how I was doing, and I said I would be doing better if I were pregnant! It was at that moment, I knew that I was ready to live my life without the pain of losing Lukas—with the hope and excitement of my future with a new baby.

So how do you move into a hopeful future? There is no plan or instruction manual. Just like the previous year, I got up each morning and lived through my day. We were living our lives as normally as we could—with moments of laughter, dreams for the future, and moments of pain and loss. We were also "trying" to have a baby. The stress of that was tremendous, not only for us, but for our friends and family. It seemed like everyone was "expectantly" awaiting our announcement. That would prove to everyone that we were "over" Lukas. It was always the big elephant in the room. Every month of not being pregnant brought me moments of intensely missing Lukas and the fear that I would never get pregnant again. I felt like I was a failure as a woman and a wife. What if Lukas was my only shot at becoming a mother? Rational or not, this was my reality. I always knew when I was ovulating, so I never took any drugs during this time, and we ALWAYS had sex based on my ovulation—whether it felt right or not. Our natural and mutually satisfying love life could be rekindled once I brought home a baby. Getting pregnant was not the total answer for me. I had proven I could do that. It seemed bringing home a living baby was the sticking point.

After about six months of no pregnancy, I went back to my same OB/GYN. I said to myself, "Why wouldn't I go back to them?" They gave me good medical care during my pregnancy, and there was nothing they could have done or known to prevent what happened to him. People tend to forget about the personal side of medicine. The "bedside manner" that, to me, is as important as good medical care. To this day, I believe if I had gotten any kind of emotional support from my doctors, perhaps my suffering would have been a little less. Included in my pain was that outrageous statement from Dr. C. Again, the words of *When Pregnancy Fails,* comes back to me, "Doctors are taught to cure, not to care." Yes, this is hindsight, and nowadays physicians are more sensitive to loss. I know that some medical schools today teach courses on loss and grief.

---SWIMMING LESSONS---

If you have a pregnancy failure of any kind, it is ok to switch physicians for your next pregnancy.

Remember, you are not just an incubator growing a human. You are a complete person who may need more than just medical care, and many physicians and their staff will be able to provide that. Listen to your inner voice.

With that being said, I did go back to the same practice, knowing I would never see Dr. C unless I absolutely had to. I met with the doctor who performed my C-section and told him about actively trying to get pregnant for the past 6 months or more. He prescribed a drug called Clomid, which I later learned was the very first step physicians would prescribe for women with "fertility" problems. Clomid is a non-steroidal fertility drug that causes the pituitary gland to release hormones needed to stimulate ovulation. I felt like this also confirmed my failure as a woman. I couldn't even get my hormones "right." It seemed like some women just look at a man and get pregnant. NOT ME. Of course, as I began the fertility work up process, I learned how many couples struggle with infertility. It may have helped me to feel less alone, but it didn't help me feel any less of a failure.

I was very fortunate and became pregnant on my first month of Clomid. We were overjoyed. I also learned the meaning of the word terrified. Now I was about to put myself to the test: Could I really go through another pregnancy, and possibly have another loss, in order to have a baby? From the moment I became pregnant, I was very sick with not just morning sickness, but all-day sickness—throwing up at any time of the day. I knew this happened, but it didn't happen with Lukas. Was this a good sign that meant I would have a different outcome and have a healthy live baby? Or was it that this "baby" was sick and wouldn't survive either? I truly didn't know what to think, and I waffled from one position to the other ... sometimes in a matter of seconds.

After about three weeks, I started spotting. I knew that I was going to lose this baby too. Yes, I know many women spot throughout their entire pregnancy and still have healthy babies, but I knew this wasn't going to be me. After two more weeks of spotting my doctor ordered an ultra sound to see what was going on with me. I was probably about 8–10 weeks along. After an excruciating wait in one of the waiting rooms in the hospital, I heard his footsteps coming down the corridor, and he walked into my room. He said the results from the ultra sound revealed that I was carrying "products of conception!" To this day, I don't know what that means scientifically, but I knew in English it meant NO BABY! I remember saying to him that I was batting 0–2 when it came to having a baby and his response was, "Well, you know, sometimes women may have six or seven losses before they have a baby!" Right then and there, I knew I would no longer be a patient of this practice again after he performed my D&C.

──────────SWIMMING LESSONS──────────

See previous lesson about changing doctors. You can change doctors at any time.

The words of *When Pregnancy Fails* returned to me immediately: "Doctors are taught to cure, not to care." and boy did this doctor learn that lesson well. Maybe he learned it from his partner, Dr. C.

Once again, we were starting our lives with no baby. My feelings of hopelessness and inadequacy returned with a vengeance. Why couldn't I do this? I felt like there was some secret password for a healthy delivery that everyone but me knew about. I knew I couldn't grieve over this baby the way I did with Lukas. Not because he/she wasn't a full-term baby or that I didn't have the same hopes and dreams for this baby as I did for Lukas, it was because now I learned I wasn't carrying a baby, but products of conception. I knew we would try again, and I needed to save my time and energy for however that was going to happen. I did give into my feelings to cry and feel the loss. To this day, I always think of this baby on his/her due date, but I knew I was going to "recover" from this loss sooner than Lukas.

I took one week off to recover before going back to work. I did have my moments of loss and pain, but I knew I couldn't "feel" it as devastatingly as I did with Lukas. Now I needed to have a baby more than ever, and I couldn't give myself the "luxury" of grieving. However, I did have a ritual with this baby. I would stroke my stomach and talk to the baby. I would tell him or her about being wanted, loved, missed, and that he or she would always be a part of our family. Again, you're told you need two months for your body to recover from a pregnancy loss, so I gave myself those two months to heal physically and emotionally. Then I became a woman on a mission! I was going to have a baby whether I gave birth to one or adopted one. I was going to be a mom with living proof to show the world that I was indeed a mother. The question became how would I accomplish that?

I decided to call Dr. H to ask for his help yet again. He told me of a new doctor that just came on staff at the hospital. He, too, was a high-risk OB doctor—a specialist in Maternal and Fetal Medicine, a Perinatologist. His patients were women with problems in their pregnancy, whether it was due to the mom's or the baby's issues. I seemed to fit the bill, so I called for an appointment. My husband and I went to see him on the very first day he had patients. We were patient number 4 that day. He listened patiently to our story, handed me tissues as I cried, and basically welcomed me to his practice. He examined me; took a detailed medical history; and said he would start us on a very basic fertility work up. He explained that he thought the first step was for me to take my temperature every morning with a basal thermometer.

A basal thermometer has a finer scale than a normal thermometer, and lets you see tiny changes in your body temperature. The process is to take your temp the first thing in the morning, before you get out of bed and at the same time each morning. Once you read the thermometer, you plot the temp on a chart, like a graph. Ovulation triggers hormonal changes and a slight rise in your body basal temp. You are looking for a pattern in the temperature rise during the time you are ovulating as compared with the previous days. If the spike occurs for three consecutive days, you are probably ovulating; if no spike, then no ovulation.

You are most fertile on the day of the temperature spike and on the few days before. The first two or three months of charting your temperature will only tell you when you have already ovulated, but you should start to see a pattern emerge, so you should be able to tell in the coming months when you are ovulating and when to have sex to maximize your potential of conception. If you do become pregnant, your temperature will stay elevated throughout your pregnancy. The one caveat to taking your temperature is if you forget to take it, or take it at a different time, or become ill, any pattern you might find may be inaccurate for that month.

I should note that this technology was state of the art in the early 1980s. Just like all technology has advanced in the last 30 years, I would think this has also.

After taking my temperature for three to five months, not only did I notice NO pattern, but the length of my period was different each month. Some months my period was 28 days; some months 38 days with a different length in between. It appeared like there might be something else wrong with me. Now I felt like I couldn't even do my period "right." Yes, my thought that Lukas was my only shot of ever having a baby was slowly becoming a self-fulfilling prophecy.

I was now referred to another kind of OB/GYN, a Reproductive Endocrinologist. Reproductive Endocrinology is a subspecialty of OB/GYN that addresses hormonal functioning as it pertains to reproduction, as well as the issue of infertility.

After several months and invasive testing, I was finally diagnosed with Polycystic Ovary Syndrome, PCOS.

What is PCOS? It is a hormonal imbalance. In women with PCOS, ovaries make more androgens than normal. Androgens are male hormones that females also make. High levels of these hormones affect the development and release of eggs during ovulation.

The ovaries, where the eggs are produced, have tiny fluid-filled sacs called follicles or cysts. As the egg grows, the follicle builds up fluid. When the egg matures, the follicle breaks open, the egg is released, and the egg travels through the fallopian tube to the uterus for fertilization. Once it "meets" with the sperm, fertilization has occurred.

In women with PCOS, the ovary doesn't make all of the hormones it needs for an egg to fully mature. The follicles may start to grow and build up fluid, but ovulation does not occur. Instead, some follicles may remain as cysts. For these reasons, ovulation does not occur, and the hormone progesterone is not made. Without progesterone, a woman's menstrual cycle is irregular or absent. Plus, the ovaries make male hormones, which also prevent ovulation.

Five to ten percent of women of childbearing age are affected by PCOS, with less than 50 percent diagnosed. PCOS is responsible for 70 percent of infertility issues in women who have difficulty ovulating. I was thinking that when I conceived Lukas, I was ovulating perfectly, and everything came together as it should. Would it ever come together for me again?

The cause for PCOS is unknown, so there currently is no cure. However, some of the symptoms that you might experience would be:

- **Irregular periods.** This is the most common characteristic. Examples include, menstrual intervals longer than 35 days; fewer than eight menstrual cycles a year; failure to menstruate for four months or longer; and prolonged periods that may be scant or heavy.
- **Acne, Excessive Hair Growth & Excessive Androgens.** Elevated levels of male hormones (androgens) may result in physical signs, such as excess facial and body hair (hirsutism), adult acne or severe adolescent acne, male-pattern baldness (androgenic alopecia), oily skin, and dandruff.
- **Problems with Ovulation-Polycystic ovaries.** Polycystic ovaries become enlarged and contain numerous small fluid-filled sacs that surround the eggs.

Although I didn't have every symptom, I had enough to know that I again won a lottery that I wasn't interested in winning!

Factors that may play a role in developing PCOS:

- **Excess insulin.** Insulin is the hormone produced in the pancreas that allows cells to use sugar (glucose). If you have insulin resistance, your ability to use insulin effectively is impaired, and your pancreas has to secrete more insulin to make glucose available to cells. Excess insulin might also affect the ovaries by increasing androgen production, which may interfere with the ovaries' ability to ovulate.

- **Low-grade inflammation.** Your body's white blood cells produce substances to fight infection in a response called inflammation. Research has shown that women with PCOS have low-grade inflammation, and that this type of low-grade inflammation stimulates polycystic ovaries to produce androgens.
- **Heredity.** If your mother or sister has PCOS, you might have a greater chance of having it, too. Researchers also are considering the possibility that certain genes are linked to PCOS.

Now that we had a diagnosis, what was the treatment, and would it lead me to get pregnant and bring a live baby home?

My OB/GYN referred me to the university-associated fertility clinic that would know how to treat these issues successfully. My hopes of getting pregnant, bringing a live baby home and "living happily ever after" felt like they might actually come true.

I made my appointment and met with the reproductive endocrinologists in their clinic office, which was packed with other "infertile" women hoping for their answer as well. The fact that there were other women in the office didn't make me feel any less of a failure as a woman. Collectively, we were all failures looking for the "holy grail" of fertility. After a review of my records, they told me that because I had gotten pregnant twice, once by myself (read no medical intervention) and once with the medical introduction of Clomid, I was a very good candidate for success. The fact that both of my pregnancies resulted in failure didn't mean anything. Fertility clinics are driven by successful pregnancies, not successful deliveries. I wasn't sure how I felt about their statement, but I knew I was going to do this regardless.

My protocol was to be treated with a drug called Pergonal, a hormonally active medicine for the treatment of fertility disturbances. My ovaries needed more stimulation so that I could produce more follicles/eggs, thereby increasing my chances of fertilization. When people hear of "fertility clinic", they think of multiple births ... twins, triplets and more. I was told I had only a 15 percent chance of having a multiple birth. In my mind, if I had a multiple birth, I could be done with this whole issue, as my husband and I wanted two children. At this point, I would be extremely grateful to have one living child. *Fertility treatments have changed in the past 35 years, and I can't address current treatments. All I can discuss is my experience.*

How would this work? For the ten days leading up to my ovulation, I would come to the clinic before I went to work. I would have my blood taken to see what my estrogen levels were. Based on those results, I would be given an intramuscular shot of Perganol to adjust the levels. Once the follicles mature, an injection of Human Chorionic Gonadotropin (hCG is a hormone that completes the final stage of egg maturation) is given to stimulate ovulation and the release of mature eggs. Sex follows, and hopefully as in my case, a pregnancy.

I had learned the hard way what was best for me (see car accident). I knew that I didn't want to hear anyone's story about why they were in the clinic; how long they had been a patient; or anything else about their history. I needed to concentrate only on why I was there. I wasn't about to take on anyone else's fears or history. I always brought a book with me and separated from anyone else. I didn't care what anyone thought of this. I was protecting myself, which was my only concern.

On the day, I was to receive my hCG shot, I was told that my levels were so low, I would never conceive. Now, wasn't that confidence-building? However, since, I had already taken all of the other shots and the blood tests, I might as well take the hCG shot and follow the protocol and have sex anyway. I said ok and thought: well maybe sex won't seem like such a chore tonight. Maybe we can be passionate like we used to be. Perhaps this would be the upside!

One of the benefits of "assisted reproductive technology" at that time (maybe it still is), is that you can find out if you are pregnant within ten days of the hCG shot. I think in 1983 it might have been 14 days. On the 14th day, almost at 5 p.m., I called the clinic to get my results … figuring another month; another failure. The doctor came on the phone and said, "Well, Mrs. Hovatter, we don't know how you did it, but you are definitely pregnant!" Stunned doesn't even begin to explain my feelings. Yes, I was excited, but now I was terrified. My mission had become my reality. However, the old family superstitions and neurosis appeared again. My first question to my doctor was nothing normal. It was, "because my levels were so low, and you said I would never conceive this month, does this mean there is something wrong with the baby?" I see now that I was always ready with a doom and gloom comment! He said, "absolutely not," and that I should go home and celebrate with my husband, family and friends. I thought much easier said than done.

Our celebration was tempered as you can imagine. Because all our friends and family knew I was going to the fertility clinic, they all were waiting for the outcome of the past month's "work." We told them we were pregnant, and the baby was due on February 15th. We were offered congratulations, and only my brother asked me how my head was about this, because he, too, is part of the doom and gloom brigade! I said I was terrified, and that if I could be induced into a coma for the next nine months, I would probably be ok! He laughed, but that was truly how I felt. However, I knew that wasn't possible, so I would have to figure out a way to "get through" this. After all, this is what I so desperately wanted and pursued like a crazy person. So, I told myself, "Yes, Nancy, figure it out."

───────SWIMMING LESSONS───────

It is not unusual to have mixed feelings of terror and joy with a subsequent pregnancy. Do not feel guilty if you are not excited.

I found myself talking to the baby and saying "I am so happy to be carrying you; you are the most wanted baby ever; but I am terrified to lose you. I may seem like I am detached, but I am so bonded to you. You will never know, but I'm so afraid to talk about you out loud. I also don't want anyone else to talk about you out loud." I thought that if it was hardly mentioned, perhaps if I lost this baby too, it wouldn't be so devastating. I also knew I was kidding myself about that. I knew I would be much worse than how I was with Lukas. For everyone reading this who has had a loss, and is now pregnant again, that is the one reality we share.

─────────────────SWIMMING LESSONS─────────────────

Be prepared to lose this baby too.

    I made my decision to have another baby, NOT based on being afraid of losing the baby, BUT on bringing the baby home. I did have to acknowledge I could lose this baby too. This baby was the only thing I cared about or thought about, but that had to be my baby's and my secret. However, I was TERRIFIED! I made my appointment with the high-risk obstetrician who had sent me to the fertility clinic. Within minutes of walking into this office, I started crying and telling him how terrified I really was. He sympathetically listened and told me he would help me however he could. I asked him about the coma, he laughed and denied my request.

    After my examination, we talked about my pregnancy in general, and what I could expect. He said that with the exception of my son's heart problem, I had no higher risk than anyone else my age for having a healthy pregnancy and baby. I would be 33 when this baby was born. I asked him if I had to have a C-section again since that was how Lukas delivered. He said no. I said I wanted a C-section because I needed to have an end date to this pregnancy.

I felt that if I knew when it would end, I could count how many more days were left in the pregnancy. I then asked him about types of testing. I asked about an amniocentesis. He said he thought I was too young, so he would send me to a geneticist and have him discuss the pros and cons of this procedure. Since my husband and I were Jewish I asked him about being tested for Tay Sachs disease. Tay-Sachs disease is a rare inherited disorder that progressively destroys nerve cells (neurons) in the brain and spinal cord and is more common in people of Eastern and Central European Jewish heritage than those with other backgrounds. My husband's father was not Jewish, so maybe this would bypass us. Again, the geneticist would help us with this.

The big question I had to ask was: Was there any testing for the baby's heart? Remember in 1980 when Lukas died, I was told there were no tests (at that time) that would pick up Hyperplastic Left Heart Syndrome. It was now 1983, and my doctor told me that there were now two hospitals on the East Coast, one at Yale in Connecticut, and one in a hospital in New York which had a new test called Fetal Echocardiogram. A specially trained ultrasound sonographer performs the test, and a pediatric cardiologist (who specializes in fetal congenital heart disease) interprets the images. My baby was the perfect candidate.

I was overjoyed. We lived in New Jersey, just over the river from New York, and I knew we would make an appointment. I would have to wait until I was 21–23 weeks pregnant because that's when the heart is big enough to see all four chambers. It was also within the legal limit to have an abortion if I chose, because HPLHS diagnosis is not compatible with life.

I had the answers to my questions, and now all I had to do was to live through the next nine months. There were only two times a day I gave into my excitement and allowed myself any relief from my fear of loss: when I got up in the morning, and when I went to sleep. I would caress my stomach and tell my baby how much I loved him/her; how wanted he/she was; how I was getting excellent medical care to assure he/she was coming home with me; and how we had made it through another day. Making it through another day meant one day closer to a delivery. I really lived this pregnancy day-by-day … and sometimes minute-by-minute.

I didn't tell anyone at my job because I was too afraid to share the news. However, at ten weeks I started spotting, so I had no choice but to tell my boss, and then go home for four weeks of bed rest. Bed rest is always instructed, but in reality, I believe there is nothing one can do to prevent a miscarriage. So, once again, here I was … possibly about to lose my baby and become a failure once more. I carried on one-way conversations with my baby all the time. "Please live!" That was my mantra. "I promise I'll be the best mother to you. I will love you unconditionally. We will be friends. Just give me the chance and survive."

I stopped spotting after two weeks, yet my fears of losing this baby remained strong. I stopped thinking about my future with this baby, because I wasn't convinced I was going to have a future with this baby. I now thought of all the other horrible stuff that can happen to a baby in its development, and how that could happen. Doom and gloom were my closest neighbors, and there were no thoughts that could make them go away. Again, a medically induced coma sounded really good at this time.

Soon, the first of the specialist appointments arrived, and we went to the geneticist. He was a lovely man who sees couples all the time to learn what genetic markers they have that could impact the outcome of a baby. After our meeting, he said we had no chance of Tay Sachs, so although I wasn't really worried about this, I could at least cross it off my list. As for the amniocentesis, he said he would advise against it. He said I was young enough (under 35) that he didn't think this baby would have any neural tube defects. He was the expert, so we decided against it. Even though we made the decision to not have the amnio, I still worried that it was the wrong decision. I also realized that no matter what decision I made about anything regarding this pregnancy, I would always second-guess myself.

My pregnancy was moving along, and my husband and I were living our lives with the big elephant (growing baby) in the room and in my belly. We hardly spoke about the baby; bought nothing for the baby; didn't discuss names; and just watched my stomach get bigger. There were moments of pure joy when the baby kicked. Of course, we would smile, put our hands on my stomach, and just hold our baby. One time the baby kicked so hard, the tiny little foot could be seen, and I could hold onto it. Even in those joyous times, I could ruin those moments by thinking, "OMG! The baby is moving too much … maybe he/she is being strangled by the umbilical cord." If the baby hadn't moved as much, I would think it had already strangled, and that was why it wasn't moving. I had no peace, and I couldn't comfort myself. The coma I mentioned earlier was the answer!

Finally, the big day of the Fetal Echocardiogram arrived. This was brand new technology, so we didn't know what to expect. Our anxiety and fears were huge. After all, this would be the moment when we would learn if our baby had the same HPLHS as Lukas, or we could finally relax and think about our future with our baby. We were led into the Ultrasound room, and my husband remained with me. We were told that the test on average takes about 45 minutes, longer depending on complexity of the baby's heart. I was on the table almost 3 hours. My baby decided to show us he/she had a mind of his/her own and would not cooperate so that all four chambers of the heart could be seen. The doctor could see three out of the four chambers (which were normal) and said if there was anything wrong with the fourth chamber, it would somehow or somewhere be seen on the other chambers. Now, do you think this brought me any comfort or relief? NO!! My glass remained half empty!

We drove home, mostly in silence. By the time we reached our home, we both knew we would continue with the pregnancy; believe what all the experts told us; wait for our healthy baby to be born, so we could bring him/her home. Maybe this time we could live happily ever after.

My pregnancy continued uneventfully, and I managed to keep my fear somewhat under control. I only felt safe in my OB's office, but the minute I walked out, I was in panic mode. We took "baby" steps in thinking about the future with this baby. We started to look at furniture again (different than what we picked out for Lukas); reviewed our Lamaze breathing; and even met with pediatricians. When it came to names, I knew I still wanted to name this baby after my mother, but I certainly wouldn't use Lukas again. The girl name we had picked out (in case he was a girl) was Lindsay. I knew that was also out. This time, I wasn't going to use the letter L as a first name. I was also going to name this baby after my grandfather Joe, so we started to look at J names for the first name, and L names for the middle name. In Judaism, you name your child in Temple with a Hebrew name (that is the one that counts), so we decided to name our child JL in English and LJ in Hebrew. What those letters would mean, we hadn't discussed.

When I was 33 weeks pregnant, my husband went with me for my OB visit because my car was in the shop. He usually didn't go with me. Fortunately, he was there because I was diagnosed with preeclampsia. Preeclampsia is a pregnancy-induced condition characterized by high blood pressure and signs of damage to another organ (often the kidneys), with protein in the urine. It can begin at any time in a pregnancy, but usually after 20 weeks. If left untreated, it can lead to serious and often fatal complications for both mom and baby. The only cure is delivery of the baby. What else could go wrong? Was I doomed to never have a baby?

From the doctor's office, I was admitted to the hospital where I stayed three days, and then discharged home on complete bed rest (other than going to the bathroom). After five days at home, I went back to my OB, and he sent me directly to the hospital to be admitted. On the way to the hospital (since it looked like we were going to have a baby), we decided that we would name the baby either Jessica Lee or Jake Lawrence. This was on a Friday. He told me if my blood pressure couldn't be controlled over the weekend, he would deliver me by C-section on Monday.

On Sunday afternoon, my OB came in and told me that nothing had changed. For my own safety and that of the baby's, he would need to deliver me the next day. I asked him what would happen once I was delivered. He told me that a neonatal fellow would attend the delivery … that was required of all C-section births to make sure the baby was ok. However, because of my history, the neonatal attending (who also was the physician for Lukas) would also be there. He said that the baby would be taken to the Intensive Care Nursery (ICN) for a precursory check since the baby would be about 5 weeks early. Because of my history, the baby's heart would be checked out. He said this was standard, and I should try to relax. Ha ha! I asked him if he could schedule the delivery as early as possible, since I was already a wreck and didn't know how much longer I could hold on to my sanity. For the first time, I really understood things being out of my control, and I did NOT like it at all. My OB came back later to tell me I was on the OR schedule for 7 a.m. the next day.

Later that afternoon, the anesthesiologist came in to discuss my epidural and how I was going to be monitored. At this point, all the physicians who were going to be in the OR knew the history of Lukas and how "crazy" I was. He assured me that once the baby was born, he would give me something to calm me down … and probably put me out. He couldn't give it to me prior to the birth, as it would affect the baby's breathing. He, too, assured me that I was receiving the best standard of care, and he would be with me every step of the way. I explained to him about my overwhelming fear of being paralyzed, and that I would wiggle my toes all the way. He laughed and said okay.

At 6 a.m. on Monday morning, January 9th, the nurses came in to prep me for delivery. My husband was with me, and to say I was nervous is quite an understatement. I was told I would be wheeled into the delivery room around 6:45 a.m., given the epidural, and then shortly thereafter my baby would be born. We waited and waited and nothing … 7 a.m. came and went. So did 8 a.m. Finally, I heard my OB's footsteps coming down the hall, and I knew this wasn't going to be good. He came in to tell me that he messed up with the schedule of the OR, and now I was scheduled for delivery around 2 p.m. I was so angry at him because of the delay. Didn't he understand that I needed this baby to be born, and I needed it to be born right now? I couldn't keep holding my breath!

Again, none of this was in my control, so all we could do was wait until the next scheduled time. Since I was already prepped there was nothing for the nursing staff to do. I couldn't eat or drink anything before the delivery. We waited and waited. I alternated between tears of frustration, fear, and then extreme anger. I told my OB I didn't want to see him again until we were both in the delivery room.

Of course, when the time came for me to be wheeled into the delivery room and given the epidural, it didn't go smoothly at all. It took him way too long to find the right spot. If I had any fear about being paralyzed before the epidural, I knew for sure that this time I was definitely going to be paralyzed. How could someone who is an expert in giving epidurals not find the right spot on my back? To me, this was all part of the same dark cloud of doom hanging over me.

Finally, we were all set. My husband was sitting at my one shoulder and the anesthesiologist at the other. My OB was wonderful and told me everything he was doing while he was doing it. My toes wiggled accordingly, so maybe paralysis wasn't imminent.

Finally, at 2:19 p.m., Jessica Lee arrived into this world at 6 lbs. 10 oz. and 18 inches long. Of course, I became hysterical ... first because I didn't hear her cry, and then when she did, I sobbed with relief. After a brief checkup, the neonatal fellow left the delivery room. The next thing I heard was, "Mr. Hovatter, Dr. H would like to see you outside for a moment."

A brief moment of joy was followed by catastrophe. I started screaming that this was happening all over. How could this be happening again? I wanted die and all sorts of other stuff. My OB instructed the anesthesiologist to give me whatever he needed to put me out but trust me when I say ... NOTHING could put me out. My adrenalin was pumping, probably into the stratosphere. My husband came back and told me that she, too, seemed to have some problems breathing, but they thought it was because it was a C-section delivery. I told him that this is exactly what was said to me before Lukas was taken away forever. I also screamed about holding this baby. Even if she was dead, she was going to be put into my arms. I was not going to have another episode like with Lukas.

My OB came over to me and spoke very quietly, which of course shut me up immediately. He said that as soon as I was all sewn up, I would be taken to the recovery room. Then, as soon as I could sit up, I would be taken to the ICN (on my gurney) to Jessica. I quieted down, and within 15 minutes I was rolled into the Recovery Room, and as soon as I was in place, I sat straight up and said, "Take me to the ICN NOW!" They finally took me to see my beautiful Jessica. In her first picture, an ICN nurse was holding her with wires hanging out of her, and then I had the most precious moment of my life ... she was placed into my aching arms. She was very alert and serenely calm. She looked up at me and seemed to say, "Relax, Ma! I'm here. I'm going to live, and you will finally have proof that you are a mom." I told her I would love her unconditionally forever and would be the best mom that anyone could want. I calmed down, and for the first time in I don't know how long, I could exhale.

At that time in the medical insurance industry, HMOs had not yet come to the East Coast, so insurance companies allowed mothers with C-sections to stay in the hospital for seven days. Babies stayed in the nursery. This turned out to be life-saving for Jessica. Early in the morning, on the fifth day of her life, I heard my OB's footsteps coming down the hall. It was very early; much too early for his rounds. I recognized his footsteps, and I knew he was coming for me. He stood in the doorway and before he spoke, I said: "Is she dead?" I was surprisingly calm, because, honestly, I really didn't expect any other answer but yes. He said no, but there was a problem. She had been transferred back to the Neonatal Intensive Care Unit (NICU). He told me that when the nursery nurse was making her rounds, she said one-minute Jessica was fine and the next she was blue, so she was transferred back to the NICU to see what was wrong. Of course, I knew it was her heart, and this was some sort of cosmic joke being played on me: letting me think I finally had a baby, only to have her die a few short days later.

Looking back, I can't imagine how I remained so calm and still stayed in my bed. I called my husband to tell him there was a problem, and he said he would be right there. About 45 minutes later, he came to the hospital, and together we walked into the NICU. I really didn't know what I would find. What I found was medical staff hovering around Jessica's isolette discussing her case. Dr. H saw us and came over. His demeanor was very calm, empathetic and sympathetic, three characteristics needed for his type of "job." He said the last thing he wanted was to see us in the NICU. He said from the initial examination and the nurses' report, we could rule out HPLHS (which of course was a relief to us). It did make us worry that it was some other life-threatening illness. He couldn't tell us how long it would take to find out whatever it was, or how long she might remain in the NICU. As soon as they had the answer, we would too. All we could do was wait.

It felt like history was repeating itself. Waiting for tests in the same hospital with the same physicians and nurses as Lukas, and not knowing what was wrong with her or what the outcome would be. As much as I was terrified, I had set myself up for this. Once I made the decision to get pregnant again, I had to be prepared to suffer another loss. There was no other option.

──────────── SWIMMING LESSONS ────────────

Once you decide to get pregnant again, you have to be prepared to lose that baby too. The desire to have a baby MUST be stronger than the fear of suffering another loss. You have to be willing to take the risk that you will lose the next baby too. Get as much information as you can about why you lost your baby, and only concentrate on that reason for your loss ... not any other medical catastrophe that could happen.

For some, this might be very hard as there are not always reasons why we have a miscarriage, stillbirth, or some sort of fetal birth defect. Even if you have a diagnosis as to the cause of your baby's death, there is still no reason why (unless you are a carrier of a specific gene that carries the birth defect) it happened to your baby. Using me as an example, I had a diagnosis for Lukas' cause of death, Hyperplastic Left Heart Syndrome. However, did I have a reason WHY that happened? No. I often thought what would have happened if I had gotten pregnant either a month before or a month after I did. Would that baby still have had HPLHS?

With my tears and fears, we returned to my room and started to make the calls to hold off on celebrations because we weren't sure we were going to bring this baby home either. We didn't know what to do. I wanted to be in the NICU sitting by Jessica's isolette, but that wasn't possible. We sat in my room and just looked at each other, really not saying anything. We were again alone with our thoughts, not being able to comfort each other.

Very slowly, we started to get some answers from the neonatologists that whatever tests they were doing were coming back negative. So far, other than turning blue (and I say that with my tongue firmly planted in my cheek), there was nothing wrong with her.

After three days in the NICU, and no definitive answer, my seven days were up. I was discharged home—yet again without a baby. Same elevator ride; same empty arms. I will say that I wasn't nearly as sad or as bereft as I was when I left the hospital after Lukas died. After all, my child was still alive, and it looked like she just might come home if we could only get a diagnosis and treatment plan.

We went home, and yes, it was as deathly quiet as it was when I came home without Lukas. Sadie was chomping at the bit to spread her love to me. I allowed it, and this time I didn't cry when she kissed me. I was excited and started talking to her about Jessica, and how Jessica was going to come home soon. I finally allowed myself to talk about my future with my daughter, although I only said it to Sadie and not to anyone else. Still no furniture delivered; no clothes put away; or no baby supplies bought.

Over the next five days, my husband went to work, and I sat on the couch. When he got home, we would go to the hospital and see Jessica. I fed her, changed her, and held her. I really was in heaven. Again, we received nothing substantial about a diagnosis, just her one "breathing episode." Finally, we were told that it looked like she had "infant apnea."

Infant apnea is the temporary suspension of breathing or rapid breathing followed by apnea. It is believed to be associated with Sudden Infant Death Syndrome (SIDS). SIDS? Crib Death? How was I going to cope with this? Dr. H said that all of Jessica's apnea tests were exactly on the fence, no definitive answer either way for apnea. They decided to err on the side of caution and treat her as if she had apnea. What this meant was that she would come home on an apnea monitor that measured her heart rate and respirations. If one of them slowed down too much, an alarm would go off. If the alarm went off, we would have to gently stimulate her, so she could regain a normal heart rate or respiratory rate. Worst case scenario, we would start CPR. On the last day of her hospitalization, my husband and I were taught infant CPR. I was so stressed thinking that I might really have to save her and give her CPR, I could feel my own heart racing! Yet, I was so excited because we were going to bring her home. Regardless of her medical condition, I was truly going to live "happily ever after" with my daughter!

Having a baby on an apnea monitor is no small thing. Yes, we knew our lives would change with a baby, but it also changes in significant ways that you would never know or even think about with a diagnosis of apnea. We were told we could only leave her with CPR-trained individuals as babysitters. My in-laws were trained in CPR. We would have to notify our local firehouse/EMT to let them know about her so if we had to call them, they knew what situation they were walking into. We also had to notify the electric and gas company that we had medical life-saving equipment in our house, so we would have to be one of the first ones to have power/gas restored in case we ever had a blackout. Because it was January, we had to notify our town, so our street could be plowed first in case the firetruck/ambulance had to come rescue Jessica. If I was driving alone with her, I had to drive in the right lane, so in case the monitor went off, I could pull off to the shoulder and administer CPR. Yet in a very strange and concrete way, I was comforted. I could feel reassured when she was sleeping that she was still breathing and alive. The monitor would tell me otherwise.

On day 11 of her life, we brought her home. I finally got to go into the hospital elevator with a baby. I didn't care about not having the balloons or flowers other moms had. I had the most important thing: a breathing, living daughter. On the way home, we stopped at Lukas' grave to introduce both of them to each other. It was something I felt so strongly about. I knew I wasn't replacing him with Jessica, and I needed to tell him that. I needed them both to know that they were brother and sister … whether he was here physically with us or not. This would be the first of many cemetery visits with her.

———————SWIMMING LESSONS———————

Many parents make the same decision to visit the cemetery. Only do this if it feels right for you.

My in-laws were waiting for us at our house for the homecoming all of us had missed the first time around. Smiles, tears of joy, and photos were the order of the day. I couldn't stop beaming at my daughter. Finally, my body did not disappoint me. Although I had never really thought about actually being a mom, what that meant, or how to be one, I just knew it was going to be the most natural state for me. All my nerves and neuroses were gone.

We also showed Sadie, our dog, her new "sister." We allowed Sadie to sniff around and even lick her because she was the newest member to the household. She came over to me with her tail wagging and started licking me, and I just knew how happy she was. The energy in the house had suddenly changed to one of life and joy. If I could feel it, I knew Sadie did too.

What I had not anticipated was the re-grieving of Lukas. Of course, there was no one to tell me that this might happen, and it wasn't until years later that I figured it out. I knew I wasn't in a postpartum depression, because I was able to function in all areas of my life. I was just sad. Years later, I realized that in the first week (and really it only lasted about a week), I finally had a baby and got to do all the real baby things moms get to do, but I never got to do with Lukas. Jessica was tangible, and what I had to do for her as her mom was also tangible. Once Lukas died, he became my thoughts of "what I could/should be doing for him." I had to imagine my interactions with him. With Jessica, there was no imagination. Without knowing it, I truly realized what I had lost.

We were finally a "family." Jessica was a very good baby and seemed to be content with whatever we did for her. It was almost like she knew that after what we went through, she would be calm, so I could relax into being her mom. Years later in speaking with other moms who had lost their babies, their subsequent baby was also calm. Maybe it was our gift from the Universe.

One of the best things I did was to find a very good pediatric group that knew my history of loss and the potential for me to probably be more nervous than other first-time moms.

SWIMMING LESSONS

Interview as many pediatricians as you need to until you find the one you are comfortable with. It is important that you share your story with him (and the other partners) so they understand why you might call more often and ask a lot more questions than other moms.

I was hoping I wouldn't let my anxiety about all the possible catastrophes that could happen blow up something minor into something major. They always made me feel like they were my partner and took the time to answer my questions—no matter how trivial they may have thought they were. There were two distinct events that clearly illustrate why they were so important to me.

When Jessica was about 6 months old, I noticed that she had blood in the corner of her eye. I knew this wasn't usual but had no idea what it was and immediately called the pediatrician. It was on a Sunday night, and I knew he would tell us to bring her to the ER (which of course we did). She had scratched the cornea of her eye, which is fairly common. The ER doc put a patch over her eye and said to keep it there for 24 hours. I would like to say I was calm throughout this, but that wouldn't be honest. I was a little crazy with all the possibilities of what it could be, and I couldn't shut that voice up. Hearing her diagnosis was a big relief. We got home from the ER around 11 p.m., and in about an hour, my pediatrician called me to make sure first off, that I was calm, and to reiterate Jessica's diagnosis and treatment.

When Jessica was about nine months old, we went in for her monthly pediatric visit. I noticed that the pediatrician was taking a very long time touching her head—much too long for my comfort. Doom and gloom had suddenly shown up in the exam room, and with a barely audible voice, I asked what was wrong. He said her "soft spot" had closed, and it was a little early to do that. I asked what that meant, and he said if it closes too soon, the brain wouldn't have enough room to grow properly and her head would be very misshaped. Still not processing what he was saying, I asked, "You mean her head will look like the Coneheads (from *Saturday Night Live*)?" He could tell I was starting to get very upset and re-explained what he had just said, this time leaving out the worst implications of what this could mean. He said she would need an X-ray of her head IMMEDIATELY. Once he had the results, he would call me and discuss them.

I left his office and went to the imaging center, crying all the way. I brought her into the office. I handed her over to the technician, and as soon as she was out of my sight, she started screaming. It was so bad and so gut wrenching for me, I had to leave the building. I knew she was going to be restrained and this must have terrified her. I went outside (crying myself) and then screamed at the gods. How could this be happening? I was not rational, but my fear was very powerful and completely and utterly out of control. Was Jessica or I being punished for something that we did or didn't do? Hadn't I already given "at the office"? Why should I have to give again—under any circumstances?

We returned home and waited for the pediatrician to call. I felt like I was waiting for an execution. He called in about an hour. As soon as I answered, he didn't announce himself, he just said, "All is Good." Another exhalation. He said that the X-ray showed there was plenty of room for her brain to expand, and we didn't have to be concerned. Happier words were never spoken.

Now, I don't know if this is how my pediatrician dealt with all of his first-time moms or not, but I know that is how he and the rest of his partners dealt with me … and that is exactly what I needed. Information, for me, is powerful. Not having it is scary. I learned that I had to advocate for my child as well as for myself.

──────────── SWIMMING LESSONS ────────────

Tell everyone how you need to be treated. That is something I continue to do to this day. I would strongly urge you to do the same.

I was quite surprised by the response I received by friends and family when I voiced complaint or exhaustion about taking care of Jessica. I was usually told, "Well, you asked for this." or something similar. What was that supposed to mean? Because Lukas died, I was never allowed to voice anything in the slightest negative about being a mom or taking care of Jessica? Why wasn't I being treated like any other new mom? It was much easier to talk to people who didn't know my history. From them I would get some sympathetic nods, hear their mommy war stories, and share some laughs.

The first year of having Jessica with us was as fantastic as the year of not having Lukas was painful. It is important for me to tell you that after the first few days of having Jessica home and missing Lukas intensely, there was never really a comparison again. She didn't live in his shadow then and doesn't now. I knew very well that they were two separate babies. For family and friends, it was very easy because after Lukas died, they never mentioned him again. For them, Jessica was definitely someone else besides being a different sex. Once again, my brother came through for me. The first time he came to visit and see Jessica, he was the one who told me she looked like Lukas, so I had some sort of framework to picture him and remember him by. My husband and I didn't discuss this because we had learned not to really speak of him to each other anymore. This was a gulf that we had a hard time bridging.

We celebrated all of the holidays that first year with Jessica. No longer were we only just observing them. Of course, Mothers' Day was fantastic. Yes, we did go to the beach for lunch, as was our tradition. This time we were just like every other family there … we had a baby, and we were a family. I got tons of cards from friends and family, even friends of my parents who I hadn't seen since I had gotten married eight years earlier. We did stop at the cemetery because I needed to have both of my children with me. Even though Jessica was way too young, I wanted her to know that she had a brother too. It was important for both my husband and me (perhaps a little more for me) for her to know her family history, and that included Lukas. We had a huge celebration for her first birthday with two separate parties in one day—one for family in the afternoon; the other for friends and neighbors at night. I became so choked up when we sang Happy Birthday, that even to this day I have a hard time with the song. It wasn't because I never got to sing it to Lukas, rather, it was because I never thought I would sing to another child of mine.

My life with Jessica was usual in all the ways of having a baby were at the time. I was a stay-at-home mom meeting other stay-at-home moms … with play dates, routine housework, etc. Every three months Jessica had an apnea sleep study, and her results were always the same: borderline, so she remained on the monitor. I used to joke that she can stay on the monitor until she gets married, so her husband can worry about her breathing! I also knew that I wasn't ready for her to come off the monitor, as the monitor comforted my neurotic self about her remembering to breathe. When she was 13 months old, I was ready, and she was free of the monitor.

When Jessica was about 14 months old, I found myself pregnant again. I absolutely couldn't believe it. In fact, I took three home pregnancy tests over three days to make sure. My fertility doctors told me it was very unlikely I would become pregnant on my own because of my PCOS. For the first time in my life, I didn't use birth control and was very relaxed about it. I was completely overjoyed and completely calm. I thought the worst was behind me. My body had finally given me a healthy baby, so my body knew how to do it. I still had fears that I would lose this baby too, or he/she would have some problem, but it was in the back of my mind, not front and central as it was with my pregnancy with Jessica. My excitement was short-lived, as right after I called my OB to make my first appointment, I started bleeding profusely and wound up meeting him in the ER. I realized I was kidding myself about being relaxed about this pregnancy. I was again terrified I would lose this one too. After an examination and an ultrasound showed I was still pregnant, neither my doctor nor I held out much hope that this pregnancy would remain viable. I was discharged home and told to wait to see which way the pregnancy would go. Once again, I was on the cusp of feeling like a failure while also "excitedly" talking to this baby about holding on because he/she was very much loved and wanted and had a sibling to meet.

Two weeks later, I finally went for my "first" OB visit in his office. The bleeding had stopped, and I started to believe I was going to have a baby. I would be 35 when this baby was born, and I was going to have an amnio. I also learned that technology had advanced in the two years since I was pregnant with Jessica.

Because a fetal echocardiogram was becoming more available, I would be having this test at the pediatric cardiologist's office down the street from my OB in NJ. In the years since, fetal echocardiograms have become the standard of care in pregnancy. At that time, it was only available to "high risk" moms who had lost a child to a fetal cardiac abnormality.

I had my amnio and learned I was having a girl, and she had no neural tube defects. The fetal echocardiogram showed her heart was perfect. Even though everything was ok, there would still be no baby things in the house and definitely no baby shower until she came home with me. However, we allowed ourselves to talk about this baby with our friends and family. We were all cautiously optimistic that this baby was coming home too.

On December 8, 1985, Brenna Michelle came into our lives. I've always said she would do great things in her life because she was in a hurry to be born. I went into labor with her at 33 weeks and managed to hold off delivering her until 34 weeks. She weighed 8 lbs. and was 19 inches long. Because she was premature, she too went into the Intensive Care Nursery, but mostly as a precaution to check her lung development. She only stayed overnight and then went to the regular nursery. We both stayed in the hospital four days, and finally, I left the hospital in the wheelchair holding a baby. Even today, when I think about that, I am brought to tears. After such a struggle, I had my babies ... my family was complete.

As we did with Jessica, we stopped at Lukas' grave to introduce them to each other. Looking back now, I realize this is how I started to incorporate him into their lives. By including the girls into our traditions and rituals for Lukas, like his birthday and lighting a memorial candle for him, we introduced them to their brother. They may not have been able to understand any of it, but it seemed important. As they got older and would ask a question, we always gave them age appropriate answers and nothing to scare them. When they each (and separately) asked the big question of what happened to him, I told them that he had a very bad booboo in his heart that could not be fixed, and he died. By that time, there were members of our family who had died, so whatever they thought death was, they just added Lukas to that mix. Our answers to their questions never scared them and satisfied their curiosity. Of course, this conversation happened when they each were about 4–6 years old.

On his birthday, we all went to the cemetery. For the girls when they were young, it was just a very nice park where mommy and daddy stood quietly for a moment. When we placed a rock on Lukas' headstone, they would also search for a pretty one and place it. I don't know if it is religiously-based, but it is Jewish tradition to leave a rock on the headstone of the deceased. I think it is to let the deceased know that they have been visited. If we told them early enough, sometimes they would color a picture and bring it to him as well.

It was during one of these times that I realized I really didn't get any comfort by visiting him or feel closer to him because I was standing above him. I realized I carried him with me all the time and could "speak" to him whenever I wanted. I didn't need to go to a certain place to be near him. He was inside of me and always with me. Yes, sometimes the pain of his loss was there, but it was the love I felt for him that comforted me. I was his mother; he was my son; and nothing would ever change that. I didn't need to go to a cemetery to be reminded of that. I also recognized that when I was feeling emotional about him in any way (sad, melancholy, etc.), it was okay, because that was the only way I could parent him. Instead of feeling dread on those special days (birthdays, etc.) or just missing him because something or someone reminded me of him, I embraced my feelings and quietly said "Hello, Lukas, so glad you could join me today."

I also didn't dwell on the girls "having to know" about Lukas. It was a gradual progression, as I said. However, there were two episodes that stand out for me that made me realize, "they know." When Brenna was about 5 years old, I asked her to set the table. She asked me for how many? I asked how many people are in our family? She counted everyone's name out loud, including Lukas, so she said five. I was touched, but kept it light and said, "Lukas would not be joining us for dinner, so please set the table for four."

When Jessica was about 6 years old, a child psychologist I knew was putting on a conference about grief. Her topic was specifically on how children, born to a family after a child has died, process this information. Jessica was asked to draw a picture of her family. She drew her parents, herself, and her sister all close together. Off to the side, she drew a crude bassinette with a baby inside. When the psychologist asked who that was, she said, "That's my brother Lukas."

When a baby dies, parents can be afraid that other family members and friends will forget him. We, as his parents, know he will never be forgotten to us. It is the outside world that doesn't mention him for fear it will be upsetting to us, which makes us think he has been forgotten. Again, I go back to the analogy of why photos of dead relatives are displayed in your home, yet when you put a photo of your dead son or daughter, people are upset and might even ask you why you have such a photo on display.

─────────────SWIMMING LESSONS─────────────

Feel free to display photos of your baby.

Family members mention dead relatives all the time when they are reminiscing. I have learned that the major difference is that the family and friends know, identify, and have shared memories and experiences with these dead relatives. For those of us who had this particular kind of loss, our friends and family don't have these memories. Maybe they never saw your baby, or you "lost" your baby during your pregnancy. They may think if you talk about this baby it will be too painful for you. They never realize what a gift they will give you if they give you permission to talk about your son or daughter.

What "others" don't know about pregnancy loss is that as soon as we find out we are pregnant, we mentally and visually have lived our entire life with this baby. We see our baby taking their first step getting their first tooth, celebrating family birthdays and holidays, going on family vacations, starting their first day at school, graduating from high school and college; walking them down the aisle, becoming grandparents, and everything else in between. Everything that we thought and hoped for is gone for us. Whether our baby is "lost" at six weeks, full term, or anywhere in between, that life that we pictured/imagined/planned is gone and can never be experienced. It doesn't matter if you have living children at home, or whether you are fortunate to have a subsequent child. Your imagined life with THAT baby is gone. How do you explain that to someone who has never experienced this? I think this is why the loss of a baby through miscarriage, stillbirth, or neonatal death is so isolating for the parent. We truly feel alone.

There will be many times (months or years later), when you least expect it that you will be reminded of your son or daughter. It might devastate you and fill with you pain, as if it was the first day after your child's death. It might also be very soon (or even years) after your loss. You weren't expecting it, and you hadn't prepared for it.

My experience with this happened in the spring of 1981, about seven months after Lukas died. I had already gone back to work, so I was with people every day (even though at the time, no one knew about Lukas). I was seemingly able to function in most areas of my life, although there were times I still cried and missed Lukas terribly. The Jewish holiday of Passover was approaching, and my uncle was diagnosed with a very rare form of cancer and given 3 months to live. My cousin, Barbara (his daughter), called me to ask me to come to my aunt's house for Passover. The whole family would be there, and this would be her dad's last time for the family to be together. They all lived in NY, but my husband and I lived in NJ. Somewhere in my mind, I knew this wasn't a good thing for me to do, but I didn't know why. I loved my cousin and loved my uncle. I said yes, as the bells and whistles were going off in my head and heart saying not to do this.

The day arrived, and off we went. What should have been about an hour and 15-minute travel time, turned into more than three hours. When we finally arrived, my aunt greeted me at the door holding her 2-year-old granddaughter with a big grin welcoming us. I know it wasn't intentional, because honestly no one understood that my husband and I were still grieving the death of Lukas; my aunt was excited to show off her granddaughter. However, I took one look and off to the bathroom I went, crying my heart and eyes out. I was just sobbing uncontrollably. My other aunt came into the bathroom and asked me what was wrong. I clearly remember saying, "Michele has her baby; I want my baby." and just sobbed more. My aunt left me alone until I was ready to come out. The rest of the afternoon was just horrible, and to top it off, they were celebrating the granddaughter's 2nd birthday … complete with a cake and the birthday song. Not only were my husband and I extremely uncomfortable, never saying a word to anyone (or each other), but we made everyone uncomfortable too. I am so sorry about that to this day.

I never thought I would have behaved that way, or that seeing my cousin's daughter would be such a crushing reminder of what I didn't have. I understood why seeing infants my son's age was painful, but I didn't expect it from seeing my cousin's child who was a 2-year-old and a girl to boot. We left as soon as the coffee was served and took another 3-hour ride home.

That was the last time I ignored my inner voice about anything concerning Lukas. It would take me much longer to follow that advice when it came to other areas of my life. Years later, I became a believer that every experience teaches us something, and nothing is a failure.

SWIMMING LESSONS

It's a matter of figuring out what you are learning from this experience, even if you can't figure it out immediately.

Eventually you will understand it. Like me, it took many years to accept and listen to what my inner voice was telling me. Once I did, my life changed tremendously.

Throughout my life, there were other "public" connections to Lukas that remain to this day. In the winter of 1980, it was the year of the winter Olympics, and the USA hockey team defeated the U.S.S.R. I remember watching all the USA hockey games; cheering them on; and wondering if my son or daughter would grow up to be a hockey player. Of course, the USA went on to win gold which is known as the "miracle on ice." Even today, when any news or sports story comes on about the team or the win, I am immediately taken back to my living room back in NJ, watching the game and rubbing my belly. My pregnancy with Lukas and the USA hockey team are woven together forever. I can't think of one without the other. I am ok with watching it now because I remember how happy I was at that time. I was excited and loved being pregnant, so I remember that feeling and smile.

The song of the summer of 1980 was the big hit "Babe" by Styx, off their album, *Cornerstone*. It seemed to be playing all the time, and to this day I remember the words. Well, when Lukas died, I couldn't listen to the song again. Just hearing the first two notes, I knew what it was and would turn the radio off. It was just too painful for me. It was many years later when I was driving home from work, it came on the radio. I remember thinking, I have to finally make peace with this song and decided to listen. I said out loud, "Okay, Lukas this is our song, so let's listen, sing, and remember our time together." Thinking about the words now, they seem to be prophetic. The words were written by Dennis DeYoung for his wife as he was packing to go on the road to perform, but it could very easily describe some of my thoughts after Lukas died. It felt like Lukas could have been singing the words to me, because he knew he was never coming home with me. He was trying to tell me that and encouraging me to be strong.

> *Babe, I'm leaving,*
> *I must be on my way.*
> *The time is drawing near*
> *My train is going*
> *I see it in your eyes*
> *The love, the need, your tears*
> *But I'll be lonely without you*
> *And I'll need your love to see me through*
> *So please believe me*
> *My heart is in your hands*
> *And I'll be missing you.*

> *'Cause you know it's you babe*
> *Whenever I get weary*
> *And I've had enough*
> *Feel like giving up*
> *You know it's you babe*
> *Giving me the courage*
> *And the strength I need*
> *Please believe that it's true*
> *Babe, I love you.*

I can now listen to the song just fine and sing every word. It is my song with Lukas, and it is our time to be close together. It now brings me comfort and smiles. Who would have guessed that?

In September 2001, Lukas would have been 21. One of the passengers on one of the planes that went into the World Trade Center lived in our town, and she, too, was 21. I don't remember how soon after the tragedy, but our town had a memorial and observance for this person. The ceremony was down by the lake, and her parents displayed their daughter's life story in photos. We saw her very first photo, first steps, first day at school, family occasions, birthdays, sports photos, and graduations from elementary, middle, high school and college. My heart ached for those parents, and I knew their grief journey would be difficult. For me, looking at those photos made me realize again the life we lost when Lukas died. Here was the life he should have had, but of course didn't. These photos could and should have been from my family, as we had photos just like them of the girls. I never thought attending this memorial service would bring me back to Lukas.

There also may come a time when you want/need to publicly acknowledge your child even many years after their death. This happened for me when Lukas would have turned 13. In the Jewish religion when a boy turns 13, he is no longer considered a minor and he is regarded as ready to observe the religious *precepts (commandments)* of the religion. He is responsible to fulfill all of the Torah's *(the first 5 books of the Hebrew scripture—Old Testament)* commandments and is eligible to take part in a public worship. We call this his bar mitzvah. The term *"bar mitzvah"* literally means "son of the mitzvah" (mitzvah—good deed or commandment).

All my life, I have read the New York Times—in particular, the columns that announce weddings, births, and the obituaries. For me, it was a glimpse into how other people lived and died, and it always seemed more interesting than my life. When the girls were born, I placed announcements of their births in the New York Times, so it only seemed natural for me to put something about Lukas as an "in memoriam" in the obituaries. I wrote: *My darling Lukas: We should be celebrating your bar mitzvah, and how I wish you were here with us. I hope you know that we love you always and will always carry you in our heart. Love Mom and Dad.* Of course, my husband knew I did this but no one else in my circle of friends and family. It was only important to me, and still is to this day. I don't think anyone who hasn't had a child die would understand why I did this… and I'm okay with that. When the milestone your child misses arises in your life, whether it be religious (like Lukas and his bar mitzvah), or socially, you do not need anyone's permission to acknowledge it.

SWIMMING LESSONS

Please give yourself permission to acknowledge your child's milestone, however brings you comfort.

You also have permission not to acknowledge it as well. It is whatever will make you feel better. It also doesn't matter how long it has been since your child has died. Perhaps the length of years makes it that more important for you. As I have said before, do whatever will bring you comfort, even if it is bittersweet.

When the time came for the girls to have their bat mitzvah, I also acknowledged Lukas during their ceremony. During every synagogue service, there comes a time when the rabbi remembers the names of the dead relatives of its members and leads the congregation in the Kaddish, or the mourner's prayer. The prayer is an expression of faith on the part of the mourner: although we are distressed, we still believe in God and in the worthwhileness of life (Jewish *Book of Why*). Every immediate family member (mourner) receives a calendar of when to say Kaddish during the first year of that person's death (usually the first 30 days), and then annually thereafter.

As we approached the time for Jessica's bat mitzvah I spoke with our rabbi and stated that when it came time for the Kaddish to be read, I wanted Lukas' name to be announced as well as my parents (even though I knew it wasn't the time for it to be said for them). I explained that my son and my parents should have been alive; and if they were, they would have been there. So, by announcing their names, I was publicly acknowledging them. I also knew this was my way of inviting them to be there. After much heated discussion, the rabbi agreed. It was a very poignant moment when their names were read. For me, it was really the first time (not counting Lukas' unveiling) that his name was said in a public setting. I saw the expression on my in-laws faces as they thought of their grandson, as well as that of my mother's family who missed my mother terribly. Lukas had been dead 15 years and my mom 20; and for one brief second, we were all together acknowledging these people and it was meaningful, beautiful, and peaceful. We did the same for Brenna's Bat Mitzvah, but this time I didn't have to argue with the rabbi.

PART II

Sharing the Life Preserver

Many bereaved parents experience what some experts call post-traumatic growth. Richard Tedeschi and Laurence Calhoun, psychologists at the University of North Carolina at Charlotte, note that positive changes often emerge after a crisis, such as greater appreciation of life and a greater sense of personal growth (NY Times, Oct 2015). Reading those sentences now, I can tell you that I wouldn't have believed it if I had read it 35 years ago. However, I know it is true for me, and I started to realize that about seven years later without knowing that exact statement. I was at home with the girls who were approaching 2 and 4 years of age. I was so in love with them and completely content. I thought about my darkest times when I thought that I would never feel this way. I remembered how I had to work through my grief alone and how difficult that was. I had experienced so much in the seven years that had passed—from the conception of Lukas, to his death; my grief journey; to my medical conditions; to getting pregnant and bringing each daughter home; to this moment in my living room with my two adorable daughters.

Perhaps I could help other parents in their journey; offer them hope and support; make their journey a little less of a struggle; take a moment to tell them it is okay to feel the way they were feeling, and most importantly, that they won't always feel this way. I wanted to show them that after this devastating loss, you can (if you chose to) have subsequent children and put your life back together. It will be different from what you thought it would be, but it can be a very happy life.

I called the NICU at the hospital where all three of my children were patients and explained who I was and what I wanted to do. I spoke with the clinical nurse specialist of the unit, and she informed me that they had just started a parental bereavement support group that met once a month. She invited me to attend the next month's meeting.

On the first Wednesday of the following month, I walked into the conference room on the second floor of the hospital to attend their parental bereavement support group. I arrived a little early, so I could meet the facilitators of the group. At this meeting, the facilitators were the clinical nurse specialist from the NICU, and the office manager/RN of the maternal/fetal physician's office (who had previously been my doctor). They told me that the group had just been formed two to three months before. The facilitators alternated each month, with these two women one month, and the perinatal social worker and another hospital staff member the following month. All the facilitators met most of the parents because their babies were either in the NICU, were patients of Dr. H (maternal/fetal specialist) or had been seen by the social worker. The group was open to all parents in the community, not only to former patients of the hospital. Since this was the 2nd or 3rd meeting of the group, and since they hadn't been facilitating at all the meetings, they couldn't tell me if there were any parents returning to the meetings.

We sat at the conference table and waited for the parents to walk in. I remember thinking how broken these people looked, almost like the "walking dead" or "zombies" in today's vernacular.

I realized I once looked like that. Their eyes were vacant; their body language defeated; their faces expressionless; and they were barely able to walk into the room. Even selecting a seat at the table seemed monumental—I felt that the room was a scary place for these parents—especially if it was their first time. They didn't know what to expect of the group, or if they "had to" participate by speaking. And what if they cried?!

The room was silent until the facilitators broke the ice. Each one introduced herself, even if they were known to the parents. They said the purpose of the group was to be a safe forum for parents to speak about what they were experiencing, and to help themselves (and each other) as they struggled with the loss of their baby. It didn't matter what their loss was, they were all grief stricken, and unfortunately, that was their commonality. The parents were told that if they didn't want to speak, they didn't have to.

I was introduced as a parent who had suffered the death of my 2-day-old son seven years prior. I told them my story. I told them how I came to be sitting in this room, starting with my pregnancy with Lukas (and of course the aspirins); his birth and transfer to the two different hospitals; and his ultimate death two days later—while I was still in another hospital in a different state. I told them what it was like to lose a baby in 1980 when no one knew what to do or say to my husband and me, including the staff from the hospital, family, or friends. I talked about how overwhelmingly isolated I felt. I told them about my mental health (about hearing Lukas cry and thinking I was going crazy); told them about my lack of concentration on the smallest of details; and how I could do nothing but sit on the couch, mindlessly petting my dog and crying, while my husband went to work. I told them how my husband and I grieved so differently that there were times I thought we would split up over Lukas. I told them how a friend of mine and I were pregnant at the same time, and because of my loss and her birth, it was too hard for me to remain friends with her. I told them that for me, having another baby was not the answer to my loss of Lukas because I wasn't emotionally ready to have another one; I still wanted Lukas. I had to experience my loss and my feelings until they weren't so devastating. I needed to work through my grief each miserable second until I knew that there was a future for me. That is what worked for me. Each of them would find out what would work for them when it came to their own grief as well as having a subsequent child.

Then I told them about Jessica and Brenna; and how we were all thriving. I told them that I needed (and wanted) to come to the group to tell them that they would survive this horrible loss; put their life back together again; and be happy—even if they couldn't believe it right now. Their lives would be different from what they thought they would be, but they would one day laugh, plan for the future, could have subsequent children and be happy. I told them it might be very hard to hear, and they may think that's not true for them, but here I sit before them as living proof that it can be done. I wanted to be their symbol of hope, and I offered my support to them to help them in any way I could through their grief journey. I wanted to be a resource for them. As I said, I was once exactly where they were.

The energy in the room shifted slightly as the parents listened to my story. I noticed some cried as they listened, some nodded and recognized themselves in my story and some just sat. Their body language opened slightly. When I was done with my story, some started talking about their loss. It didn't matter if their loss was a miscarriage during their pregnancy, a very premature birth, a stillbirth, or neonatal death; all the parents had complete sympathy and empathy for the other person, and thought their loss was just as horrible as their own. No one loss was valued more than the other, nor was an early pregnancy loss dismissed as "just a miscarriage." They all understood, and each "got" where the other person was at the time. I did too; I also knew what they were going to be facing.

When the meeting was over, some parents came up to me to thank me for coming to the meeting. They shared how hearing my story helped them—whether it was hearing how I got through "it," knowing I got through "it," or hearing about getting pregnant again. Some asked specific questions about an experience, dream, or conversation they had. They asked if I would come back to the next month's meeting, and I agreed. I also spoke with the facilitators at the end of the meeting, and they said that my presence at the meeting made a tremendous difference in the group dynamics. They, too, asked me to return the following month, and I said I would.

Two different facilitators ran the next month's meeting. Some of the parents had returned, and unfortunately, new bereaved parents also attended. The facilitators introduced themselves and stated their position at the hospital; then I spoke. I told my story again. There were some new parents in the group, while others from the previous month returned. Although it was very easy and unemotional for me to tell my story, I realized that I had never really told "strangers" my story before. The friends and family who knew my story, really only knew that Lukas was born and then he died. No one really knew what I experienced, and seven years later I was finally stating exactly what it was like to live as me during that year. It was very cathartic for me. I realized that although I was at the group to help newly bereaved parents, in my own way, I was also helping myself.

I returned the next month, and the facilitators who were at my first meeting were there. I recognized some of the same parents from the previous months, and of course, new "members" walked in. The facilitators waited until everyone seemed to be settled, and then the introductions began. It was always the same. The hospital people just stated their name and what they did, and then I spoke and told my story. Once I was finished, there was always silence as I watched the parents work up their courage to speak and tell their story. Eventually parents who had been at the previous month's meeting spoke first, and then one or two new parents would speak. Their grief was the same, only the details of their loss were different.

One mom started to speak and told how she was reorganizing her closet when she came upon a photo of her son who had died about 4 months previously. This mom and dad had been to all the meetings I attended. They had a 4-year-old son and a home. She said that when she looked at the photo, she burst into tears; threw the photo against the wall; then all the photos of her "dead" son against the wall; then slowly everything in the closet was thrown; then almost everything within reach of where she was standing was thrown. She was stunned and ashamed that she had done this. When she was finished speaking, there was absolute silence in the room. I knew why she had done this, and I was waiting for the facilitators who were "professionals" to comment. When they, too, sat in silence, I spoke up. I said I thought she was angry about the death of her son and that's ok. She had every right to be angry. I thought the reason she was throwing the photos was because she realized these would be the only photos she would ever have of her son—not the usual photos of him growing up. Why wouldn't she be angry? Who wouldn't be angry that their child died?

Just like that, the other parents started talking about their anger, their jealousy of seeing other parents with their babies, their lack of concentration, their hopelessness, their joyless life, and every other emotion they were experiencing. They started expressing their outrage over some of the comments they received … how no one understood what they were going through, etc. They also asked me questions directly about how I handled certain situations. The big question was always: When will I stop feeling like this? My answer to that question was always the same: When you have done your grief work. You have to explore and inhabit each feeling that you are experiencing, so you can let it go. You may have to work through the same feelings many times, but eventually you will release it and be free of it. There is no easy way to do grief work: again, you have to live through each miserable second. Think of it as a ring of fire. You are standing at the outside of the ring when you are pregnant, you jump through the ring when your baby dies, and you remain in the ring until you are "ready" to come out the other side. No one can pull you through to the other side. You have to jump out.

When the meeting was over, the facilitators and I spoke again. They said they were going to have a meeting with the other facilitators and would like me to attend. I agreed. A few days later, I attended the meeting with all four of the facilitators. The two facilitators who were at the last meeting explained what happened to the two who weren't there. They said they realized that the group was working so much better with me there than when they first started. They thought it would be best if I attended every meeting, because it was obvious that the parents were getting so much more from me than them. I had the experience, the knowledge, and the words, to really work with these parents. I agreed to their offer to become the parent facilitator. I then said I thought it would be best if they decided amongst themselves which one of them would attend every meeting, because I thought it was important for the parents to have consistency and continuity.

I know for me, if I had someone who knew my story of Lukas and I spent time with them every month, they would see the progress I was making in assimilating my loss into my life … even when I couldn't. I thought this was very important, so I wouldn't feel alone. The perinatal social worker said she would be the other facilitator of the group, as she was the one who saw the parents in the hospital after their loss, including the ER. The Social Worker told the parents about the group. She said she led it along with a mother whose son died at two days old. She assured the parents that the group was a safe place. I think the parents were grateful to know she would be a familiar face in the room, as well as having a mom who also lost her baby. She would understand what they were experiencing. I think these two things made it less scary for them to attend. I agreed to be the parent facilitator with the perinatal social worker. This is how I started working with the bereaved.

On the first Wednesday of the month, the perinatal social worker and I facilitated the parents' bereavement group. Each month as new parents walked in, I was heartbroken for them, yet so glad they had a place to come to. This group was going to help them, so they wouldn't have to walk the same lonely path I had walked. I was going to walk with them, comfort them, listen to them, and help them heal.

The process of the group was always the same. The social worker introduced herself by name and title, and then I spoke. Before I launched into my story, I would tell them that this group and room was a very safe place; that their participation in the group was strictly voluntary; and if they didn't want to speak that was ok, as no one (neither the social worker nor myself) would call on them to speak. In the first few months, I was very "chatty" when I told my story. I told them practically everything I had said the first time I spoke at the group. When I look back on it now, I think I had to do that, as I was never really "allowed" to tell that part of my grief. Besides, who would I tell it to? Once the girls came along, no one thought about Lukas or all the "trouble" I had before them. By talking about my experience with Lukas and with my grief, I was finally able to bring him into the world by acknowledging him and what I went through. In that room, just as I had said to the parents, you could talk about your baby all you wanted … no one would stop you. In that room, we were the "normal" ones and not the outsiders. In that room, we all had a shared experience and identity, even if our babies were different. Unfortunately, we were members of a "secret" club that no one wanted to join; but we would learn how to help each other heal, so we could join (or rejoin) the "mommy club."

Very slowly, I stepped into the "leadership" role of facilitating the group. Unfortunately for me, I had become the "expert" in how to work through grief after losing a baby. It was my "gift" … although a gift I never wanted. I knew I could help these parents, and I did help them from the first meeting I attended. It was my honor, even my pleasure, to help them. If I could help one person to suffer even one minute less, then I was successful.

The parents I had met in the three meetings I had attended returned, and of course new parents always walked in. The social worker and I fell into very comfortable roles: her as the professional "expert", and me as the parental "expert." Most of the parents she had met in the hospital and knew their story. We never knew who was going to attend the meeting because we didn't ask for any kind of registration or to call ahead. The nature of support groups is usually on a drop-in or need basis, and sometimes parents didn't know they needed to come until the moment they walked into the room. Other times, parents would drive up to the hospital intending to come to the meeting but couldn't get out of car because they associated the hospital with their baby's death, and that was just too painful at that moment.

I also noted that most parents' first meeting was usually two or three months after their baby died or their miscarriage. The first few weeks after losing your baby you are still in shock. Your body has put you on automatic pilot, and you do everything you need to do—whether it be to plan and attend your baby's funeral, take care of the children at home; or recover from childbirth or miscarriage. You may have fleeting moments of intense loss and pain, but because you have other things to take care of, your subconscious gives you some peace before reality kicks in. When that reality does set in, you are punched in the gut and you realize you may not want to do this alone. The need to know you are not alone and do have some place to tell your story is usually much greater than the fear of actually sharing it. At that point, you walk into the support group either with your partner or alone.

The social worker and I were very compatible, both on a social level and while we were working in the group. When she met with the parents, she told them about the group and that she co-led it with me. She explained that I had a baby that died and was now working with parents to help them. She also asked if they wanted a call from me, so I could talk to them on a personal level, sort of mom to mom, with an invitation to attend the group. When I spoke with the mom, my purpose was to offer my sympathies and let them tell me their story. I would share my story briefly, explain why I was doing the group, and invite them when they were ready. I usually gave them my number, so they could call me whenever they felt the need and as often as they wanted.

After speaking with the parents, I would follow up with the social worker to tell her about my conversation with the bereaved mom and my general impressions. Before our monthly meeting, we would have dinner together and talk about new parents she had met with (even if I had spoken to them); then discuss how we thought the parents who had been attending for a while were doing. Although I had no clinical training in social work, family therapy, or psychology, I instinctively knew if the parents were "appropriate." Maybe I compared them to me. Just by listening to what they were saying and how they were saying it, gave me a clue how they were incorporating their loss into their life. The social worker, of course, had the expert training, and we agreed on our "feelings."

I then learned the term "complicated grief," which I had never heard before. The short explanation is that you get stuck in your grief and don't move along processing the death. In fact, your grief even gets worse.

In writing this book, I looked up the clinical definition of complicated grief and its symptoms on the Mayo Clinic website:

During the first few months after a loss, many signs and symptoms of normal grief are the same as those of complicated grief. However, while normal grief symptoms gradually start to fade over time, those of complicated grief linger or get worse. Complicated grief is like being in an ongoing, heightened state of mourning that keeps you from healing.

Signs and symptoms of complicated grief may include:

- Intense sorrow and pain at the thought of your loved one
- Focus on little else but your loved one's death
- Extreme focus on reminders of the loved one or excessive avoidance of reminders
- Intense and persistent longing or pining for the deceased
- Problems accepting the death
- Numbness or detachment
- Bitterness about your loss
- Feeling that life holds no meaning or purpose
- Irritability or agitation
- Lack of trust in others
- Inability to enjoy life or think back on positive experiences with your loved one

When to see a doctor

Call your doctor if you've recently lost a loved one and feel such profound disbelief, hopelessness, or intense yearning for your loved one that you can't function in daily life, or if intense grief doesn't improve over time.

Specifically, you may benefit from professional help if, over time, you continue to:

- Have trouble carrying out normal routines
- Withdraw from social activities
- Experience depression or deep sadness
- Have thoughts of guilt or self-blame
- Believe that you did something wrong or could have prevented the death

- Have lost your sense of purpose in life
- Feel life isn't worth living without your loved one
- Wish you had died along with your loved one.

Now, looking at the signs of when to seek professional help, I see myself very clearly in almost all the examples. In fact, I almost look like a textbook example. One reason I didn't seek professional help is because I didn't think my feelings would be validated. After all, we were repeatedly told: "we were young;" "could have other children;" and "to just stop thinking of it and move on." I didn't think a therapist would validate my loss or my feelings. Also, at that time, there really wasn't any kind of awareness of bereavement as a mental health issue, because child death had been so common not long before. Women, and most especially men, weren't given the time or "comfort" to grieve their children because life was much harder, and the medical standard of care was completely different. So, I muddled through.

SWIMMING LESSONS

Avail from all the help that is out there.

Do not let pride or discouragement keep you from seeking help from professionals trained to help you through the grieving process.

While working with parents, we did have some parents who were experiencing complicated grief, and we knew we had to offer them some professional help. At the end of the meeting, we would ask the parents to stay just a little longer; speak with them about our concern; and offer them the list of practitioners we compiled. We stressed that we thought they needed a little more support than the group was able to give and thought it would be beneficial to their healing process if they visited with one of the therapists. We also stressed that they were still welcome to attend the monthly meetings whether they saw the therapist or not, and we wouldn't mention this conversation to anyone else.

One positive difference I think our group had from other groups that were starting to form was that from time to time, we invited extended family members to attend a specific meeting. This included grandparents and siblings of the parents. The grandparents, aunts and uncles are suffering over the loss of their grandchild, niece or nephew, and are doubly hit by watching their children and siblings suffer. They can't fix this. Some grandparents may have had their own baby die or miscarried, but the "advice" they received at that time was probably to put it behind them and move forward. Maybe they even said that to their own children. Some of these grandparents who attended did talk about their loss, and you could see on their faces the relief they felt after finally telling their story, regardless how long ago.

The main reason the grandparents and siblings attended was to see how they could help their children. For some parents, it was the first time they talked in detail about their loss and how they were feeling to their parents. It was also a safe place for them to talk about what they needed, or what the family was saying or doing that wasn't helpful. I think for the grandparents, it was an eye-opening experience to hear other bereaved parents tell their story, and to share the same kinds of feelings and behaviors their children were expressing and experiencing. I always thought it was like third party validation from another bereaved parent. The other parents affirmed their child's reaction to their loss, and perhaps now they could be more supportive.

There was no fee for attending the group. The Social Work Department paid for the social worker's time at the meeting, the meeting room rental, and refreshments. We knew we wanted to offer more than just the meeting, so we would have to do some fundraising. We started very small by leaving a cup out, and at the end of the meeting, asking for voluntary donations so we could buy a camera and film to use for photos of our fetal demises and stillborn babies to give to those parents. We also wanted to create a lending library for the parents use. We were successful in those endeavors. We also created a newsletter for the parents, in which we had a column, **In Memoriam,** and a place where friends and family could make donations in their baby's name. In the beginning, the social worker and I wrote all of the articles. In time, some parents contributed. We also held very basic fundraising events like a bake sale.

The social worker and I also worked on creating a memory box for the parents. It would include: the baby's footprints, photos, swaddling blanket, perhaps an ID bracelet, a lock of hair, and anything else the baby touched at the hospital. This would be their child's "life" and the only concrete items they would ever have of their child.

About two years after the group started, some of our parents started getting pregnant again. At first, they attended the bereavement group, but it soon became obvious that this wasn't a good fit (mainly because there were always newly bereaved parents at the meetings who were not in the right frame of mind to hear about a new pregnancy). Plus, the newly pregnant parents' fears and concerns were very different from the grief they experienced with their loss. They needed a safe place to discuss this pregnancy and all the emotions involved in it. So, *Pregnant Again* was born, facilitated by the social worker and me.

Being pregnant after a loss is very different from a pregnancy after a live birth. What can make it even harder is the lack of support the parent can receive, in addition to their overwhelming emotion of fear. A subsequent pregnancy shows the outside world that you are "over it" (the death of your baby or miscarriage), not realizing the terror you might feel is overwhelming. I remember people telling me "to just relax" and "lightening won't strike twice." My response was always, "well, why did lightening even strike once?" Some parents might also feel very conflicted and guilty about a subsequent pregnancy, like they are betraying their dead baby in order to have a live baby. They have little excitement and are afraid to bond, fearing this baby is going to die too. If they sat in the bereavement group, they now knew a host of other ways babies can die, not just the way their baby died. Remember, I wanted to be in a coma to get through it, and so did many of these parents. Once again, I told them at *Pregnant Again* what I went through to have Jessica and Brenna. I told them about the fear of losing them, especially after I had a miscarriage between Lukas and Jessica. I also told them that my desire to have a baby was so strong I was willing to take the risk of another loss, and by them sitting in this room, so were they. I strongly advised them to only think about the reason why *their* baby died, and not what else they heard in the bereavement group. We discussed thoughtless comments made to them and the responses.

A big topic was whether to use the same name again for the new baby. Naming anything is highly personal, and that was something each of us who have a subsequent pregnancy has to grapple with. For me, I didn't do it, although I did name Jessica after the same people I named Lukas for. My advice was that this is a new individual who doesn't come as a replacement for your other child but stands in your family in its own rightful place. Each family will have to come to their own answer about this.

We were always overjoyed when a new safe arrival was born. Some of the parents continued to come to either the bereavement group or *Pregnant Again* to offer support and hope, just as I was doing. Some parents we never heard from again, and that was okay too. They needed to move on from the pain of loss and focus on the joy of birth and living. Sometimes parents would come back on the anniversary of their baby's birth or death because they knew they could and would be welcomed to talk about him or her. This might be the only time and place they could.

About seven years after the bereavement group was started I started a second group at a second hospital. When I went back to work in 1988, the girls were 2 and 4 years old. Ironically, I went to work for the neonatologists who provided medical care to all three of my children. They were now at another hospital. I remember coming in for the interview to be the administrative coordinator of their office and bringing photos of the girls along with my resume. It was very rewarding to them to see how they were growing and thriving.

It was at this hospital that, along with the perinatal social worker, we started the second bereavement group. The NICU at this hospital was one of the largest ones in the state. The hospital also had a maternal-fetal OB/GYN department for high-risk women, as well as a genetics department for parents who had or were afraid they had genes that could lead to fatalities in their babies. Unfortunately, there was a strong need for a bereavement group here.

Since I was already out on Wednesday nights for the other two groups and the girls and my husband had their time together on those nights, we had this group meet on the 2nd Wednesday of the month. Just like I did with the other social worker, this social worker and I had dinner before the meeting as well. It was our chance to talk about who she had seen in the hospital; thought might be coming to the meeting; if she had any contact with parents during the weeks between the meetings; if I had spoken to any parents in the interim as well; and if and when either of us should step into the conversation when the parent was speaking.

The social worker and I ran this meeting exactly the same way as I did at the other hospital. By this time, care of the bereaved was talked about, and more and more support groups and other resources were appearing. Baby packets were already instituted here. There were now bereavement conferences all over the country, both for parents and professionals who worked with the bereaved.

Some medical schools were instituting one "grief and bereavement" class for their students. Personal stories and books were being written, as well as the beginning of art therapy—a form of "grief resolution." There were book publishers who only produced books on grief. There were coloring books and other resources for older siblings of the baby who died. However, even with all these resources and support available for the bereaved, the parents still had to do their grief work; that was what the group did. We also started a *Pregnant Again* support group at this second hospital.

October has been designated as Pregnancy and Infant Loss Month (along with Breast Cancer Awareness), and the social worker and I would plan something to memorialize the parents' loss. This would usually be the month when we would open the group meeting to extended family members. One year, we held a memorial service. We would have special articles in our newsletter. We would ask the parents what would be meaningful to them, and we would see that it happened.

PART III

Riding the Waves of Grief

As I mentioned, October is also Breast Cancer Awareness month. At the end of October in 1997, I went to the radiology department of my hospital to have my mammogram. After having multiple slides of my breast taken and waiting more than two hours for the results, the clinical nurse specialist (a dear friend), and the radiologist (who had read all of my other mammograms and I knew from the hospital) walked into my room. One look of their faces and I knew. I had just won another lottery!

Very calmly they told me about the spot they saw under my left breast. It was so small that it couldn't be felt but was definitely there. I would need a biopsy to determine whether it was cancer. The radiologist said that most tumors have definite margins, but mine was different. Mine was perfectly round on 50 percent and very diffuse (like an electrical shock) for the other 50 percent, so only a biopsy could tell. Of course, I was very shaken, and although the Radiologist kept saying nothing definite could be stated by the mammogram, I said to him, "You've seen hundreds if not thousands of mammograms, so I know you know already what it is, so tell me." He said cancer. So now I knew. I then said I didn't think I was in the frame of mind at that minute to make the calls to get a surgeon or do whatever I would have to do. I asked her to see if she could arrange for the surgery as quickly as possible. She said she would take care of everything and she did.

I went back to the office to tell my boss, and since it was already late, I left to go home. I called my husband on the way home to inform him, and to tell him I would speak to the girls when I got home. My mother-in-law had a mastectomy 11 years prior, so the girls were familiar with breast cancer. She was thriving, and although the word cancer is very scary, I hoped they would keep her in mind as I told them. On the hour drive home, I formulated what I would tell the girls. I would tell them they could ask any question at any time—no matter what the question entailed. They were turning 12 and 14.

I then had a long talk with myself about how I was going to handle this, regardless of what the biopsy said. The first thing I said to myself was that I am not going to die from this. My family dies from heart disease! I then said that I wasn't going to think about the worst-case scenario until I knew it was the worst case. I was not going to drive myself crazy about the "what ifs." I also knew I was not taking anyone's advice on how I should I handle this.

SWIMMING LESSONS

You are in charge of your medical care as well as your mental health.

Friends and family would know how to support me, because I was going to tell them what I needed from them. I was never clearer about anything than I was about this. My husband and I spoke to the girls, and they were scared I would die. I answered all their questions the best I could. I told them that we wouldn't know anything for sure until after my surgery, so we'd do the best we could to hold off on worrying until then.

On November 3, 1997 (five days after my mammogram), I had a lumpectomy, and 12 lymph nodes were removed from under my armpit to see if the cancer had spread. The tumor was malignant, but the surgeon told me my lymph nodes looked clear. It was an outpatient surgery, and when we came home, we told the girls the truth and again allowed them to ask their questions. I also told them that their lives were not going to change that much. Their job was to go to school and do their homework. They would still have to clean their rooms and empty the dishwasher. Daddy would go to work, and I would stay home to get better. The big bonus of this was that they didn't have to go to daycare because I would be home for 6 weeks. They could sleep a little later and come home right after school.

About a month after my surgery, I met with an oncologist who I knew from the hospital. He studied my results and told me that my cancer was Stage 1, and the size of my tumor was a little bit smaller than the fingernail on my pinky. He said I would be perfectly fine if I did nothing and just went on Tamoxifin (drug for women and men diagnosed with hormone-receptor-positive, early-stage breast cancer after surgery), or possibly chemotherapy and radiation to reduce the risk of the cancer coming back. I asked him about chemotherapy and radiation. He said I could do that, too, and have the same results as taking only the Tamoxifin. After much consideration and discussion with my husband, I decided to do it all, chemotherapy and radiation followed by Tamoxifin. Of course, I was scared. The deciding factor to me was the age of the girls (12 and 14), and how much mothering I thought they still needed. I also thought I would feel more empowered, like I was fighting off the cancer, and fighting for my life if I did both. And, that's what I did.

About a month after my surgery, I started chemotherapy. I was to have 12 infusions, one a week for two consecutive weeks, followed by nothing for three weeks. I had my infusions on

Tuesdays, and I scheduled them before work. No one can tell you how your body will react to chemotherapy. My doctor told me that I wasn't getting the strongest chemotherapy, the one where you lose all your hair and throw up for hours and days. I was getting a less toxic formula and would not lose my hair. It would become thinner and I probably would be the only one to notice.

As we were discussing my treatment, I asked where I would be infused in the office. He had a treatment room with lazy boy chairs for the patients to "relax." I asked him if I had to sit there, or if I could have my infusion in a separate exam room. I told him that I didn't want to be in a room with the other patients who were being treated for different types of cancers. I didn't want to listen to their war stories: what they had; how they found it; any surgeries they needed; how long it took them to be diagnosed; or how long they had it, etc. I just wanted to come to the office, get hooked up, read a magazine or book, and then go on my merry way. I think that he understood this really wasn't up for discussion, and he agreed.

―――――――――――SWIMMING LESSONS―――――――――――

Take control of what you can control, so you won't feel as afraid and vulnerable. Afraid and vulnerable is exactly how I felt when I lost Lukas, and I wouldn't feel that way again.

I always told my family, friends and office when my chemo days were scheduled. I would come to the office about an hour late and then just dig in. Everyone was so kind and loving to me; I will never forget it. By this time, I had been working there for ten years, and I considered them family. Everyone had gone through some "stuff" (divorces or deaths of parents or siblings), and we all seemed to rally around each other; this time was no exception. My brother and very close friends would always call me on Tuesday nights or

Wednesdays to see if I was having any reactions to the chemo and of course, to ask how was my "head."

I can honestly say that because I knew I wasn't going to die from this, I was really "ok" with having breast cancer. I protected myself by not reading anything about breast cancer, new treatments/drug therapies, or any personal stories. I had complete confidence in my doctors and their treatment. I wasn't going to second-guess them or myself. When I decided to go all in with this treatment, I took back the power to take control of my life.

My main concern was always the girls and how they were handling this. As a first proactive step, I called the principals of their school to tell them my diagnosis. I wanted their teachers to be aware in case their grades suddenly dropped, or they started acting out in some way. I did the same thing at their religious school. Fortunately, problems never happened. I also told the parents of their closest friends. I was completely open about everything that had to do with my disease and treatment. Everyone knew they could come to me with any question, at any time. Of course, because I continued to work and live my life as before, they did the same.

My infusions were really uneventful until I had six of them. By the Thursday of the second week, I started to have terrible stomach issues and was extremely exhausted; I was fortunate enough to be able to take those Fridays off. I would tell the girls I wasn't feeling well. I know that scared them because I think they thought it was the cancer, and not the treatment. I would always have to reassure them that it was the medicine. I would walk them to the bus stop, come back to the house, and stay in bed until they got home. I was always dressed and downstairs, so when they came home I looked "normal", and they could relax.

When I got to work after my 12th infusion, there was a celebration to mark the completion of my chemotherapy. Co-workers told me how proud they all were of me for how I got through it. I was proud of me too, because although at times I was scared and feeling sick, I lived my life as if I wasn't in treatment. I just gave myself some grace; was gentle with myself; and allowed myself to be and feel how I was feeling. I expressed my feelings to whomever I needed to and said what I needed to say. My medical "voice" was loud and strong. I think this was another step in toward developing my voice in other areas of my life, even though I wasn't completely aware of it at that time.

One month after chemotherapy ended, my radiation began. This was done at my hospital. I would get to work at 8 a.m., and then go down to radiology at 8:30 a.m. to be blasted. Once again, I didn't sit in the radiation room with the other breast cancer ladies. Even though all the women had breast cancer, they were all at different days in their radiation treatment. I was told I would have 35 radiation sessions, which came out to be every day, five days a week for seven weeks. Once again, I didn't want to hear anyone else's war stories about their breast cancer. I knew my doctor's plan, and that was all that was important to me. So, I sat in a different section of the common waiting area, reading and waiting my turn. Then I went upstairs to my office and worked for the rest of the day. Radiation makes you exhausted, too, and I took days off as I needed to.

Through it all, I lived my life. Once I was diagnosed, I decided I was not going to be identified as a cancer patient. There was so much more to me than just this disease. I didn't want to be known as "cancer patient Nancy." I was Nancy, who was being treated for breast cancer. There is a tremendous difference in those two sentences, and I was living the second one. I also continued to lead all four bereavement groups, as a second *Pregnant Again* group had been added at the second hospital (before my diagnosis). Working with bereaved parents was very life-affirming for me, because I was helping them put their lives back together and move forward to create a new life. I, too, was a creating a new life for myself as a breast cancer survivor.

One month into my chemotherapy we went out to California for a family bar mitzvah. All my life, I wanted to live there, and I remember thinking at 10 years of age: someday I'll move there. I don't know what about California had attracted me so much. I just knew I needed to be there; it was where I belonged. To this day, I can't tell you why. Thinking now, I have a very adult reason: it is because it is still the West, and it is a place where people can "reinvent" themselves. Remember, it was Horace Greely who said, "Go west, young man." Go to the West and start over. At 10 years old, I just knew I wanted to go there.

My husband had been stationed out here when he was in the Navy in the late '60s. My brother and his wife had relocated to CA in 1995. We talked about moving here right after we got married in 1976, but we never did. We came out in 1997 for the family bar mitzvah, and by the time we had walked around for the afternoon, we decided we would move by the summer of 1999 (mainly because Brenna's bat mitzvah was in December 1998).

However, the real reason we moved was because I was 18 months out of treatment for my breast cancer. When we came for the family bar mitzvah in December 1997, I only had my lumpectomy and one chemotherapy treatment. I was looking at 11 more chemotherapy treatments and then 30–35 radiation sessions. I remember my surgeon telling me that we don't stop living our lives if we have cancer. Of course, that's easier said than done—particularly if your stage of cancer is grave (stage 3 or 4). I was fortunate I had stage 1 breast cancer. I thought cancer was giving me a way to start my life all over again. More like I imagined it; wanted it to be; and I wanted it to be in CA.

I also realized that I had been touched. I had seen my mortality just like the psychologists Tedeschi and Laurence Calhoun reported: positive changes often emerge after a crisis. My decision to do chemotherapy and radiation empowered me—not only to "fight" the cancer, but to act on my dream and make it a reality. If we didn't move to California now, we would never do it; that wasn't something I was prepared to give up. This was the biggest and longest-held dream of my life, and although I didn't realize it then, it was at that moment when I learned another Swimming Lesson.

―――――――――― SWIMMING LESSONS ――――――――――

You are never too old to start over or follow your dream. You can do it as many times as you need or want to.

That seed had been implanted, and very slowly it would grow until I could no longer ignore it in all the other areas of my life.

My husband was able to get transferred with his company, and in June of 1999 we became residents of CA. I've never looked back. Of course, Lukas was still in New Jersey where he remains today. We did go to the cemetery before we left, but once again, I didn't get any comfort from the visit. I always felt worse. I would stare so hard at his stone my head would hurt. I felt so much better just thinking about him—even when I was sad or missing him. I knew the only way I would continue to parent my son was through my emotions. That made me feel better than standing over him at the cemetery.

One day while unpacking our "stuff" we had shipped from NJ, I found a manila envelope that wasn't labeled. When I opened it, I found it contained all my letters to Lukas (the only ones I saved). I hadn't written to him in years because I didn't need to. I had learned to say my thoughts out loud as if we were having a conversation. As an aside, I recently met with a woman whose two sons died, one as a 4-year-old and one as a 30+ year-old. She told me that she, too, wrote letters to her sons, but she also replied as she thought her sons would have. She said that helped her greatly. I never thought of doing that.

SWIMMING LESSONS

Writing letters or journaling can be a great resource to working through your feelings.

I sat down on the deck and re-read every letter I had written to Lukas after that terrible car accident. There were several from the first two to three years when I was missing him intensely and having a very difficult time getting pregnant. Even today, I can picture myself exactly where I was in NJ, and how I was feeling when I was writing to him. Sitting in the chair reading the letters, I felt so close to Lukas right then and there in CA. While I read them, I could see how much progress I was making in assimilating his death into my life. By reading those letters again, I had brought Lukas with me to California. I once again had my three children with me.

Our lives were pretty uneventful in CA. The girls graduated high school and went to college in CA. I had various corporate jobs … always working in hospitals. My husband remained in the food industry. We bought and sold two houses and had downsized once the girls seemed to be settled.

Although I was happy in my corporate jobs, I realized I had reached the "ceiling" in my profession and in my salary. I was an executive assistant, and my positions were assisting C-suite professionals. I was happy in my positions, but I wanted more. I wanted more money to give me more discretionary spending. I don't believe money makes us happy, but money gives us freedom to choose whatever we want … and THAT is what makes us happy.

I had noticed that one of my neighbors worked largely from home, unless she was teaching music at the local university. She invited me to a "skin care demonstration party" at her house. I got the dates mixed up and wound up at her house the day after the "party." She was able to give me a facial with the products she was selling. I had never heard of the company. I liked the way my face looked and felt, so I bought some of the products. I also took home some information to read about her company and its products. I thought I would just be a user of the products, however after using the products and seeing some improvement in my skin, as well as reading the material from her company, I decided to sell it.

I had just stepped into the direct sales or multi-level marketing industry. I had absolutely no idea what that was, how it worked, or what to do. I knew that direct sales involved selling directly to the customers without a retail shop. I connected direct sales to Avon and Amway. I had no idea direct selling was a multi-billion-dollar worldwide industry, how it worked, or how people made money from this. I decided to participate in this without doing any kind of research about the company or its products, which was a huge mistake. Before I agreed to "buy in" and become a distributor selling products, I should have researched the company: how long it had been in business, what their products were made from, how many products they had, what price did they sell for, how I was compensated, etc. I was so naïve about this. I think I was very much blinded about the compensation. I chose to overlook the hard work and learning curve it would take to be successful.

Wikipedia defines multi-level marketing as a **controversial** marketing strategy in which the sales force is compensated not only for sales they generate, but also for the sales of the other salespeople that they recruit to be part of their team. Now, not only would I have to learn all about the company and its products and everything else related to selling, but I would also have to find people who would be interested in doing this as well. I quickly learned that in this industry, the key to earning substantial money was to build a team: the more people you recruited and the higher you went in the selling structure, the more you were compensated with actual dollars as well as bonuses like trips and cars.

It was a herculean task, and truthfully, I was terrible at it. I kept trying, but I really never got any better at it. I was nervous whenever

I spoke to anyone. I was "trained" in how to sell my products, but not in how to sell other products, the company, or on how to become a distributor. I was very discouraged, but I kept thinking of all the "money" I could make, if I could only find the right people. What I didn't realize then, is that I had to become the "right" person to sell this.

I don't remember how I found the book, *What To Say When You Talk to Yourself,* by Shad Helmstetter, Ph.D. Dr. Helmstetter holds a doctoral degree in motivational psychology, is a research behaviorist, and is the pioneer in self-talk. Dr. Helmstetter says that by the time we have reached 18 years old, we have heard the word no, can't or don't 148,000 times. The majority of the information that we receive from others and from ourselves is negative, and because we have so many more negative thoughts than positive ones, the brain will always believe the most dominant thoughts.

To quote the most meaningful part of his book to me:

"You will become what you think about most; your success or failure in anything large or small will depend on your programming—what you accept from others, and what you say when you talk to yourself. […]

It is no longer a success theory; it is a simple, but powerful, fact. Neither luck nor desire have the slightest thing to do with it. It makes no difference whether we believe it or not. The brain simply believes what you tell it most. And what you tell it about you, it will create. It has no choice." (Page 25)

I seemed to have learned my programming very well from my parents, family, teachers, friends, co-workers, spouse, etc. I had "programmed" myself into believing every negative thing I was, lacked, or was too much of (too tall, too heavy, not graceful, not feminine, not lovable, too loud, too clumsy, not smart enough, didn't deserve to be happy, etc.). So, who really was I? Although Dr. Helmstetter lists five ways to come out of this negative self-talk and to replace it with positive self-talk, for me it was like reading Greek.

I understood his five steps, but it was the "how" of me really doing it that made it sound too preposterous. Could I talk myself into becoming "another" person, who was positive and optimistic … especially when I didn't believe anything I would say? That was not in my "scope" as we say today. I always believed that I had to see something to believe it; he was saying to believe (the positive self-talk), and then you will see it in all areas of your life. For me, at that time of my life, it was impossible (that would be another way of negative self-talk: I can't). However, he and the book planted a seed in my mind, and I would think about it a lot through the years.

---------- **SWIMMING LESSONS** ----------

Look for books that share wisdom and inspire you into taking different action.

I am positive that reading that book was the first step in my thousand-mile journey of becoming the Nancy I am today.

I attended sales training seminars, as well as regional and the annual training conferences for my skin care company. It was just like Dr. Helmstetter wrote. If you become very enthusiastic about what you are hearing and learning, you can maintain that enthusiasm for a short period of time before you revert to the way you were. Why? Because you still have all of that negative self-talk. Maybe he had me in mind when he wrote that.

I continued to struggle to sell my skin care products, because all I could see was the compensation I could earn if I could become successful. This is definitely the wrong reason to do anything. I had run out of people I knew to talk to about my products, so I had to find new people. I had heard about an internet organization called Meetup.com, which lists groups for every kind of interest anyone could possibly have in all parts of the country. You search for listed topics or put in your own area of interest and your zip code, and groups just pop up. I started to look for women's groups and/or business groups, so I could meet other people. My hope was that they would be interested in my products and want to either buy from me, or even become a member of my team and sell them too. Of course, that was the exact thinking of every other person in the room. However, I did meet some very interesting people, and today … 12 years later, they are still friends of mine.

One woman I met was very different. She was the organizer of the meeting and that night, I was the only other person there. Instead of canceling the meeting, we just talked. There was something very different about her. She was brimming with confidence—not just about her group, but also about every aspect of her life. We talked about my business and how I was trying to grow it. Within 10 minutes she had drawn a diagram of everything I could do to be more successful and grow my business. I was dumbfounded and in awe (and of course, completely paralyzed with fear about implementing any of her suggestions). My negative self-talk was so loud in my head, I'm surprised she didn't hear it. At the end of the meeting, I asked her about her attitude and how she learned to have so much confidence, but more importantly, her attitude of "you can do it." She told me about a course she had taken at Landmark Education. She said there was an introductory meeting coming up in a month and she invited me to attend with her. I had never heard of Landmark. All she could tell me was that it was learning a different way to be. It was about creating possibilities in your life.

I went to the introductory seminar to learn about their first course, Landmark Forum. I met some extraordinary people at the introduction. Of course, the room is filled with graduates of the course who all said it was the best thing they ever did. They also told their stories of how they were in some kind of a rut, but after taking the course, they were able to climb out of it and live the life they wanted. Their thinking about themselves, their experiences, their relationships, and their environment shifted. It was all about living a rich and fulfilling life. So here I was, many years after reading *What To Say When You Talk To Yourself*, and really no further along in my "personal development" or sales career. I was still so full of negativity about myself and the choices or options I had in my life. I felt I had nothing to lose but three days of my time. I signed up to take the course.

I had no expectations of what I was going to hear or what, if any, results I would take away from the three days. I was hoping for step-by-step instruction on how to "shift" my life. The stories I heard from the graduates at the introductory meeting and after reading their promotional flyers, sounded too abstract for me to understand exactly how it worked. I was wondering and worrying if I would understand what the leader was saying; and if I could, how I would apply it to my life?

On the first day, I arrived and looked terrified just like the other students. There were rows of empty seats (no tables), and just like the parents entering the bereavement support group for the first time, people trying to strategically sit in the right seat. Once the leader walked in, the first thing he said was that all spouses and friends that came together must split up and sit next to a stranger. We would be partnering up for certain exercises. For us to be honest with ourselves, it would be better to share our answers with someone we didn't know. He also saw the terrified look on our faces. He immediately put us at ease with some jokes and told us the background of how he had come to be up on the stage. I automatically liked him.

I did not get step-by-step instructions on how to shift my life. As a matter of fact, we weren't allowed to take any notes at all. If you asked me then what I did learn during these three days, the only thing I could really say concretely was that I had built my entire life's identity based upon one or two episodes that happened to me when I was a child. I interpreted the facts negatively. I gave that negativity much more meaning than the actual experience. I finally knew where all my self-talk came from. I had taught it to myself based upon how I interpreted (or internalized) the initial negative things that were said to me and everything else that came after. Landmark suggests we see these self-invented meanings as our "identity," and we live our life accordingly. My lightbulb went off during one of the exercises, and I could see clearly how I took one experience I had with my parents when I was very young. I had turned it into the person, full of self-doubt and fear, who was sitting in the room. I had created my entire life based on that interaction, whether it was choosing my spouse, career, or any other decision I had to make. I had learned this lesson really well. I would get to figure out the difference between the facts of the experience, and why and how I gave it such meaning. Then I could stop doing it.

If you ask me now (ten years later), what else I learned in those three days, I would say I did learn to "shift" my life. I've been living it for the past ten years but have been aware of it perhaps for the last six. When I first took the course, I was looking for step-by-step how-to instructions. I didn't get that. What I would say now is that what I experienced seeped into my being and started making its mark on me ... mostly without me being aware of it. I can absolutely tell you that writing this book is a direct result of my Landmark course.

The day after the seminar, I attended a new networking group meeting. From the description I read, it sounded different from the other groups I had attended. It was a "mastermind" group, based on Napoleon Hill's book *Think and Grow Rich*. Napoleon Hill was an early producer of personal-success literature. *Think and Grow Rich* was written in the '30s and has sold 30 million copies to date. People in the self-help/personal success industry call it their bible. In this book, Hill introduces the term mastermind.

In layman's terms, masterminding is when people get together in a group setting and offer brainstorming ideas, education and accountability to each other. Members talk about the challenges they are facing in their professional and personal life, with the goal being to achieve success in the areas you are there to "fix." Joining a mastermind group requires commitment to attendance, willingness to hear and take advice and criticism, and the ability to work with honesty, respect and support for each member.

Of course, now I needed to learn what I could about Napoleon Hill and read this book. Everyone in the group was very familiar with both. I bought the book immediately after the meeting and sat down to read it in its entirety. He has 13 success principles for living, but his overall philosophy can be summed up in one simple sentence:

"*If you can conceive it and believe it, you can achieve it.*"

My negative self-talk and thinking led me to believe that I couldn't think of anything positive about myself, so I didn't believe I could do anything successfully. I was a walking opposite statement. Now I had confirmations from three different sources that it was my negative thinking that was preventing me from doing things I wanted to do, not the circumstances of my life. I really had to look at my life and wonder how I could be such an advocate for myself, my children's (total care) and my husband when it came to their medical care, but not for myself in any other area of my life.

The *Meet and Grow Rich* networking meeting was very different from the ones I had attended previously because it was more than people networking to sell their products. It examined where we were in our life both personally and professionally and helped us move "forward into our future." This group was more about our ideas. The organizer of this group, Dr. Janet Woods, is a trusted adviser to C-suite executives, entrepreneurs, and individuals. She is the founder of the Art of Life, and director of the Art of Life Institute, where the focus is to inspire people to act on their goals, dreams and life purpose. She empowers people with tools and processes that allow them to stand in their power, aligning with their true self and embracing life on their own terms.

Prior to my taking the Landmark course, I had started my own networking group with another woman I had met at a different networking meeting. Still thinking the reason I wasn't successful in my skin care business was because I hadn't found the right people, this other woman and I started our own. I thought new and different people would come to this meeting and would be the "right" people for me. I'm sure you can guess what happened. New women showed up to this group, but always with the same intention: get more clients and business builders for themselves. I knew I needed to find some different kind of networking group, so that is how I found *Meet and Grow Rich* group. I somehow knew that this would be the meeting that would change my negative self-talk and thinking.

In my own group, we started having discussion topics, as well as traditional business networking. The other organizer and I would alternate being the speaker. The one thing I brought to the group from my corporate life was that before any meeting started, someone always read a motivational or inspiration quote. I decided to carry on with this, and before every meeting I read whatever I found that "spoke" to me. We usually discussed what had just been read; how they were interpreting it; or what it meant to them.

As I look back on that now, that was how I actively began to end my negative self-talk and begin my positive self-talk. I was told how much the reading was liked, and how glad they were that I found it. It was a success at every meeting. The funny thing is that when you create something, just by sheer ownership, you are looked at as an expert. Looking through the eyes of the members, I was suddenly an expert in network marketing, and motivational or inspirational sayings. How could I be an expert of anything, especially when it came to business or networking meetings, when my skin care business was still not successful after so many years? Yet, here I was, opening each meeting with a reading, speaking, or teaching on relevant topics, and being asked for advice on some area of their business. A "baby" expert was being born, and the negative talk was very slowly dissolving.

Janet started attending my group meetings to support me, as well as to let others know what she did, and I continued to attend hers. We also became very good friends, and still are. I was always impressed with her positive demeanor on just about everything. I wondered how she got that way ... and could she "teach" that positive personality to me? I was still looking for an instructional manual, not realizing that it had to come from beliefs within me.

While my networking group was growing, and I was cautiously stepping into being a leader, my body was starting to send me symptoms that there was something wrong. I was getting bloody blisters in my mouth for no apparent reason. Once the blisters broke in my mouth, that skin would just peel away. The blisters appeared randomly, and it didn't matter what I ate or how long it had been between breakouts. After several weeks of this, I went to my doctor. He examined me and sent me to the lab for blood tests. Ten vials of blood were taken from me, and they all came back normal. Meanwhile the blisters kept appearing. My doctor had no answer and thus I began doctor shopping to find out what was going on with me. I am a strong advocate for my medical care, so when one doctor didn't have an answer, I requested to go to another one in a different specialty. After some misdiagnoses, I was finally sent to a dermatologist since my skin was affected. I received a very lackadaisical examination. He confirmed what the rheumatologist said. Don't ask me how, but I just knew they were both wrong. I finally told him to sit up and listen to me or that I was going to walk out of his office. After I again told him my symptoms and the medication the rheumatologist put me on, he still agreed with her findings. He said that medication should have resolved my blisters within 24 hours. Here I was, ten days later, still with the same symptoms. That's when he sat up! He then realized we had something different on our hands, so he took a more thorough medical history, and then a biopsy of my gums, since it was always my mouth that was affected. He said I would hear from him in about two weeks.

They didn't call. When I called for the results, I was told to make an appointment to discuss them with the doctor. I refused. I wanted him on the phone. They refused. We went back and forth many times with each of us holding adamantly to our position. I asked her whether it was cancer and she said no. Big relief! I asked, "You could tell me what it isn't, but you won't tell me what it is?" I then told her I wasn't coming in to speak with the doctor until I knew what it was. If he didn't want to tell me on the phone, I would have my records sent to another dermatologist or my primary care doctor. As patients, our medical records are ours. We have a right to every one of them. He finally got on the phone and told me I had a rare autoimmune disease called Pemphigus Vulgaris. I asked him if it was fatal. He said no, but management and treatment could be difficult. I said, "OK" and then I made the appointment to come in.

Pemphigus vulgaris is a rare, severe autoimmune disease in which blisters of varying sizes break out on the skin, the lining of the mouth, the genitals, and other mucous membranes. **Pemphigus vulgaris** occurs when the immune system mistakenly attacks proteins in the upper layers of the skin.

In layman terms, my body attacks the glue that holds the cells together. Pemphigus is so rare it is on the National Organization of Rare Disease scale. After many quiet years, I won another lottery.

Treatment is a course of steroids. Prednisone is the steroid of choice, along with another drug that is usually used for anti-rejection of kidney transplants. Prednisone is what I call the angel/devil drug. The angelic side gets your body quickly into control usually stopping the lesions. If you are having any pain (which I didn't have), it stops that as well. The devil is the horrible side effects: mainly weight gain, insatiable hunger, boundless energy requiring little to no sleep, and insomnia.

Rather than go into the details of this illness and how I coped with it, I will say that I have had it for 11 years, am currently in remission, and not on any medication. In the beginning, I had a difficult time because of how the drugs were affecting me. My doctor offered no help in this matter, and I knew that once I could find someone else who would treat me as a whole person (not just as the illness), I would leave. I left him after four years and a second round of the disease. There is no cure, just remission. A Pemphigus doctor from Northern California, who is one of the "gurus" of the disease, had just relocated to University of Irvine's dermatology department in Southern California. I have been his patient for the last seven years, and we get along very well.

At our first appointment, I told him about myself and the most recent "flare up" with the disease. Most importantly (at least to me), I spoke about how I needed to be treated as his patient. I said my commitment to him as a patient would be 100 percent compliance, and his commitment to me would have to be 100 percent compliance with the truth. I believe that patients have to take some responsibility for their medical care, and that means asking questions of the doctor about recommended courses of treatment and medication. I said I knew he was the expert in the field, however, I had to know what was going on with my illness at all times, so I would be asking questions and expecting the truth—not the answers he thinks I wanted to hear. I did not want protection from the truth. For me, information is power and that is what helps me cope with medical problems. I had enough experience with "catastrophes" to know this about myself.

After a few weeks of being released from the hospital while I was deep in my pain and grief over Lukas, it seemed my family always had suggestions about what I should do to "get better." However, because I didn't know any different and they were older, and I assumed wiser, I thought they knew best, so I listened. That's why I went for the job interview and had a terrible car crash. That's why I took some temporary office jobs. That's why I would go to the movies by myself just to get out of the house. However, after each suggestion, I didn't feel any better. My thoughts were still with Lukas, and I knew these suggestions were all wrong. I knew what I needed. Other than Lukas, I needed to be just as I was. I knew from then on, I wouldn't take anyone's advice/suggestions blindly. I would question them about everything and see if their answers felt right for me. I also knew that after my experience with Dr. C asking me if I was breastfeeding two days after Lukas died, I would be especially vocal with how I wanted to be treated as their patient, knowing that if they weren't on board with me about this, I wouldn't be their patient.

This was probably my most profound "aha" Swimming Lesson. I had not only imagined the worst-case scenario with the aspirins and breast cancer, but I had lived it. No more. The fear of me imagining the worst-case scenario was paralyzing. I have learned that I can cope with the truth and live with the reality of my medical situation. He agreed, and in the eight years I have been his patient, I have only reminded him of our agreement once or twice. Each time he would get a little sparkle in his eye, laugh, and say, "of course."

While I was being treated, I lived my life. I worked, was a wife and mother, and ran my networking group. After several months, I knew that my "partnership" with the woman I ran the networking group with was not going to work out. We parted, not so amicably, I'm sorry to say. Janet encouraged me to continue leading the group and agreed to assist me as co-leader. She kept assuring me I could do this while my negative self-talk kept saying, "No, you can't." I didn't think I had the skills or confidence to be a leader. I thought the success of the group was due to the other person's leadership, definitely not mine. After considering this for a few days (basically on Janet's faith in me), I said yes, albeit trembling with fear.

After a brief hiatus, the group returned. Janet was the "social media" person who posted our meetings in Meetup, Facebook, and every other social media platform. Again, I thought I didn't have the skills to do this. My immediate response to learning something new, especially technology wise, had always been NO. I was always afraid of making some fatal mistake and being a failure. My negative self-talk was always with me. And why shouldn't it be? My biggest failures in life were thinking that the aspirins I took caused the death of Lukas; how my body continued to fail me with a miscarriage; and my fertility struggle to get pregnant with Jessica. I had no confidence in my ability to learn something new, when I didn't see myself as a "normal" woman. Today, I would say my Swimming Lesson would be: **Rather than allowing my negative self-talk into my head, I should have looked at how brave I was to persevere and have a child.**

At one of our meetings, we held a contest to rename the group and it became **Ladies First Business Network.** We were teaching and providing great resources for building a business, and we found that because we had such a presence on Meetup (500 women members), we were invited to other women's meetings to be speakers on women's groups. We were recognized as leaders. Dove soap contacted us as part of their girls' self-esteem campaign. Their goal was to teach girls to reach their full potential through self-esteem education and to show them that they were much more than their appearance. For two years, we held a one-day conference on the topics of building girls' self-esteem and how to build positive self-talk. The irony of me talking about positive self-talk after all my years of negative self-talk was not lost on me. We also had representatives from well-known training and self-development organizations contact us to speak at our meetings.

I found great satisfaction in leading the women in discussions. The more active I became in the group, the less I did my skin care business. I was becoming very passionate about helping other women succeed. Although I was still negative self-talking/thinking, I could now recognize it when it occurred. When I was with Janet and I said something negative about myself, she would always say to me, "What would happen if you didn't think that?", or "What would your life be like if you didn't think that?" It would stop me in my tracks, make me think of the alternative; and in turn, see the possibility of living my life in a positive way. I started to have confidence in Janet's confidence in my leadership. I also started accepting and believing the compliments that were given to me, instead of dismissing them out of hand with some negative or sarcastic response which has been another step in releasing my negative self-talk.

My greater passion was the group: working with and empowering women to grow professionally and personally. My focus was no longer on my skin care business, but on the group and meeting other businesswomen to see how we could partner with each other to be successful. I found that I was very good at this, and even started to get some women clients to coach. I seemed to have found my calling … perhaps I should have trained to be a teacher when I went off to college. At that time, there was no other option but to teach in a school, and I wanted nothing to do with that. However, here I was teaching other women on all kinds of topics, and they were not only grateful, they were teachable. They incorporated what I "taught" them into their business and into their lives. My belief in myself and my positive self-talk was outweighing my negative self-talk. I could see a different life for myself. I couldn't verbalize or visualize exactly what that was. I just knew something else was out there.

I was feeling fulfilled in ways I hadn't felt before. For so much of my life, I focused on having children and then raising them. I didn't focus on myself. While this wasn't unusual, I never thought I could do anything else. The only area in my life that I was very sure and confident in was mothering. I was, and am, a great mother.

I always thought my husband was supportive of what I was doing, but he wasn't. He couldn't come out and tell me. He always had a cynical and sarcastic streak. The comments he made about my new adventures probably contributed to my negative self-talk.

A week before our 36th wedding anniversary (and 38 years of being together), we were out to dinner. As I was getting happier with my life and myself, my husband was getting progressively unhappier with his life and his job. I thought his unhappiness was mainly due to his job, as there were major changes taking place. Every day when he came home, he talked about them and how angry he was, because he had to implement the changes without believing in them. He talked about retiring, but he wasn't old enough. We were coming out of an 18-month period of unemployment for me. We had used up all of our savings and most of my retirement account. He had brought up retirement about two months prior, and I was adamantly against it. We had a very loud and nasty argument. As we did throughout our marriage, we resolved nothing, and didn't talk about it again. I felt like we had crossed some line in our marriage. It just felt different. However, at this dinner we didn't discuss his retirement, we talked about different job possibilities for him. I knew how unhappy he was, so I suggested he find a new job, which he nixed saying he was too old. My thought was if he was willing to retire on his measly social security, let him take a different job at lower pay, because obviously money wasn't his motivation. Then

I suggested he speak with his boss about working four days a week and reducing his pay by 20 percent. He said he was thinking about doing that.

Out of the blue, he announced that he didn't want to be married to me anymore and didn't want to be with me. He was unhappy with me as well as his job. My immediate reaction was "OK." In my heart of hearts, I really was OK with this. For so many months, my husband kept saying we were on different paths. When I would ask him to explain what that meant, he couldn't or wouldn't. Looking back on this now, I can tell you what I think he was talking about.

Due to my direct selling businesses and my successful women's networking group, I grew in my self-confidence and self-esteem. My negative self-talk had mostly disappeared. I was slowly changing into a different Nancy, one that he didn't recognize and apparently didn't like or feel comfortable with anymore. It wasn't obvious to me, but I have to assume it was obvious to him. In trying to explain this, I would say I was a caterpillar in the larva (cocoon) finally, slowly metamorphosing into the butterfly. Although he might have been in the larva with me, he was choosing to stay as a caterpillar. I was spreading my wings to see the world, and to see who Nancy was as the butterfly. I knew who she was as a caterpillar, and although it may have taken 60+ years to leave the cocoon, I was leaving it and never going back.

Before he moved out I tried to have some conversations about what happened to us, and why he wanted to end our marriage. However, he wouldn't say anything other than "maybe someday I'll be able to talk about it." I did ask him if there was someone else, and he said no. I asked him if he wanted to go into marriage counseling to work on saving our marriage, and he said no. So, there was nothing to be done, but to watch him move out. About four months later, I found out that there was indeed someone else.

His first wife from over 40 years ago. They had reconnected through Facebook. All those Saturdays when he told me he was volunteering as a docent at the museum, he was really spending time with her. He did retire, and together they moved back to New Jersey—one town over from the town we had lived in. He went back to what was familiar, and to this day remains in the cocoon, while I have become the beautiful butterfly!

Even though I really was OK with the ending of my marriage, I still had to mourn the death of it, and once again walk the walk of grieving alone. Because of my well-worn experience with grief (whether it was with the death of Lukas, my breast cancer, or my autoimmune disease), I knew myself well enough to know that I would come through this and land on my feet. I had learned how to swim. I knew I would need to re-examine my married life: the choices we made together as a couple and the ones I made individually, to see if I could pinpoint how we arrived at that point. I knew it would be hard and painful, yet I knew it was the only way I would be able to move forward and start my life again.

———————SWIMMING LESSONS———————

Live through each emotion until you are done with it.

I knew there would be no time limit on how long this process would take. It would take as long as I needed it to take. I would have to be proactive in sharing my feelings with friends and family, as well as telling them the best way to support me.

I knew that I would write letters to my husband about my feelings regarding how and why he left me, and how he didn't tell me the truth about his "girlfriend." I would probably rehash some of the other issues in our marriage, and of course how I was feeling all about this. I didn't know if I would send any of them, but knew I had to write them.

SWIMMING LESSONS

Writing letters can be very healing.

The letters have been very healing for me, as I learned during my grief time with Lukas. It was the way I could release my feelings and move on.

Letter writing (and journaling) is about helping the writer to feel better, and to explore, honor, and then release the feelings being experienced. It may take many letters over a period of time to let them all go. It's not about the person you are writing to, or their reaction to it. In those letters, I learned to speak my voice for my medical care, and I was finally going to speak my voice about how I was going to live my life. Through writing, I was going to figure out how I would "recover" from the grief of my divorce.

I remained in the same place we were living. Again, from my experience and with working with other bereaved families, the worst time to make any major life change is immediately after a catastrophe. Because we had moved often, even within California, I had no great emotional attachment to the place I was living—whether it was with or without my husband. Besides, no matter where I would move to, I would take myself along with all of my emotions. It wasn't the environment I had to change, but it was me who would have to reassemble my life as a single person now; it didn't matter where I would live. Where I lived was convenient to my job, friends, family, and shopping, so why move? I would live with the ghosts of my marriage and soon to be ex-husband.

My days weren't really that different. I went to work; came home; and repeated the next day. The first day coming home after my husband moved out was stressful. One of my friends asked me if I wanted her to meet me, so I didn't have to enter an empty house. I said no, because I would have to face it eventually. I felt very anxious as I drove home, but once I entered my place, I felt fine and at peace. I knew then I was going to be fine and I am.

It's been four years since that dinner, and yes, it was hard. There are still some tough times today. Living alone, I had plenty of time to relive our arguments and their non-resolution, only to have the same ones with the same results. I questioned myself continuously. Why didn't I fight harder for the things I felt were right? I questioned my judgment, my decisions, and the consequences of each action. I realized it is very easy to be a "Monday morning quarterback." That was what I was doing by looking at my marriage through the prism of who I was today. I was now Nancy the butterfly; not Nancy the frightened, weak, non-confident woman who didn't think anything good was possible for her. With this insight, I learned how to forgive myself for all of this, and to forgive him for walking out. I worked on these issues and resolved them through my tears, my letter writing, and my continuous conversations with my friends and myself. Interesting, isn't it, that I handled this grief just like I handled my grief over Lukas? I never would have imagined what a great trainer my son would be throughout my life.

I also returned to the sanctuary of my car which had served me so well when I was grief stricken over Lukas. Except this time, I didn't cry; I drove in silence and didn't turn the radio on. I found I liked the quiet of my car—where I could hear my thoughts and didn't have to hide them. I could have an out loud conversation with myself about what I was thinking. That was very healing, and to this day, the radio doesn't play too often when I am in the car.

I finally did send my husband a letter. Over the months, I rewrote it many times until it said exactly what I wanted it to say. I requested he not respond, because there was nothing he could say to defend or justify anything I had written him. About a year later, I moved into my own apartment. It was the first time in nearly 40 years I lived alone. I was excited by the thought. I remember when the movers had put the last of my boxes and furniture into the van, I looked around and took a nice deep breath. I said out loud, "OK, all of my crap and negativity about myself and my husband are gone, and I'm not taking it with me to my new place or into my new life I am creating." And I haven't.

What is my life like today? I have challenges, as we all do. I am very happy, grateful, and appreciative of every new opportunity that comes my way. I know that the life and belief system I once had is gone, although negative thoughts still pop up. I guess the big difference is I don't let them linger. I explore what it is I am doing that causes me to think like that. It is usually something I am frightened about. Once I can figure that out, I talk myself out of it.

During my thoughtful moments about the future, the question always comes up: What do I want to do with my life? What I realized is that I have learned so much about myself, and it all started when Lukas died, when I had to figure out a way to live my life without him. It was an awful struggle, but I did it; I turned my life into one that is filled with confidence, self-esteem, joy, love, and happiness. What I want to do is to show families that they, too, can put their lives back together, and even improve upon them after the death of their baby. I used to tell parents that at some point in their lives, they will identify something and know that "it" happened because their baby died. It will be something that they can look at as a positive outcome. Something will have changed about them for the better (maybe more patient, insightful, etc.). Because of the way I was, and the way I am today, I know that if I can do it, people reading this book can also do it.

Through my own history and my 12 years of working with bereaved families, I know there is much work that still needs to be done. I want to continue to work with bereaved parents and do it on a larger scale.

When Lukas died, I thought my world died with him, never thinking that I would be happy again or have subsequent children.

As you have read, it hasn't been easy. Thirty+ years later, I can't imagine it any other way.

Do I still think about Lukas? Of course, but not every day. Do I still miss him? Of course. The impact of his short 2-day life became my life's story. It is because of his birth and death, I became the person I am today—from the depths of despair to the joys of my life. Most people want to know that when they die, they have left some sort of legacy. His short 2-day life was his legacy to me, and it changed me forever. Consequently, all the bereaved families I work with will also be changed for the better, because of his short life. If that was his mission, then he was successful.

My wish is the same for you. You can "recover" from the death of your baby and have a joyous and wonderful life, just as I have. Hold onto that thought and believe it.

Jump through that ring of fire to the other side and begin your life again.

Nancy's Nuggets

Over the course of 30 years of working with bereaved parents, and through my own personal experience, I've listed below some suggestions that helped me, as well as the families I worked with along this journey.

1. There is no right or wrong way to grieve.
2. Grief is universal. We all grieve differently. Acknowledge, respect, and accept the way your partner is grieving, even if you don't like it or understand it. Even though you both have shared the same exact experience together, your reactions may be very different. This can be based on how each of you reacted to other catastrophes in your life, or how your family showed you their reactions to their losses. Just like viewing a movie together or reading the same book, you both may have different reactions to it.
3. Name your baby and refer to him/her by name rather than saying the "baby." Each time you refer to your baby by name, you make him/her real, giving him/her identity, and acknowledging that he/she is a member of your family. Also, if you refer to this baby as the "baby," when and if you become pregnant again, no one will know which baby you are referring to.

4. If you took photographs of your baby, please feel free to display them. This baby is a member of your family, and you have every right to show him/her in your family history. It will probably make some people uncomfortable, and you might even get some comments about displaying a photo of your "dead baby." Remember that families display photographs of their dead parents, grandparents, etc. all the time. No one is uncomfortable with those. The difference is that your loss is very tragic, and it makes people uncomfortable. Plus, they may have never seen your baby, and usually don't know what to say or do.
5. When you are ready, have a follow-up meeting(s) with your obstetrician or neonatologist to answer all your questions. Write them down before you go and write down the answers you receive. This will help you remember what was said. If you had an autopsy performed, have the doctor review it with you at that meeting. Ask about genetic testing, or what, if anything, can be done the next time to prevent the same thing from happening.
6. Join a bereavement support group even if your partner doesn't want to. Support groups help you to feel less alone and that you are not the only one who has experienced this loss. It can be very comforting to hear your words and feelings coming out of one of the other parent's mouths. From my personal experience, I can tell you that a support group is a very safe place to speak about your feelings, your baby, and whatever else you need to say (as often as you need to say it). Most people in that room have been where you are. It is also good to see other people further along in their journey and know it does get easier. It can also be used as a point of validation to friends and family by saying, "someone in my support group said." That is what we call third party validation and it can be more believable and powerful to your friends and family than if you say the exact same thing.

7. See a therapist if you feel overwhelmed, even while attending a support group. You are bereaved and may need help to cope. It is a sign of good mental health to know you need help to feel better. You also don't have to tell anyone about seeing a therapist. Again, do whatever you need to do to feel better. If you are using alcohol or drugs to numb your pain, you have reached the time to find a therapist.
8. Be honest with friends and family about how you feel, especially if someone has said something hurtful to you. You can just tell them that their comment, although well intentioned, is not helpful or comforting.
9. If people ask you what they can do to help, find something for them to do. It can be very simple, like picking up the dry cleaning, bringing the trash containers to the curb, picking up or taking your older kids to an activity, picking up something from the grocery, etc. You'd be surprised how someone else completing these small tasks can give you a sense of space and freedom lessening your load. It will also make the helper feel like they are doing something for you.
10. In the very beginning, set a time to do the exact same thing at the same time every day. Nothing big. Maybe brush your teeth, take a shower, or have a cup of coffee—it doesn't have to be anything too taxing or exhausting. What this does is give you a break from your grief, because you know at 7:15 a.m., you are taking a shower. For those few minutes, your mind is thinking/waiting for the time to do the activity. Perhaps during that time, you are not thinking of your loss. It can be a break from your grief.
11. Don't take the nursery down or put away your maternity clothes until you are ready, even if family/friends think it would be a good idea. I wouldn't recommend that you let anyone do it for you or without you. They may think that you will feel better if there are no reminders of the baby, however, only you know

what will make you feel better. If you can go into the nursery and it brings you comfort, then keep it for as long as you need to.

12. Try journaling your feelings or writing letters. As I said in this book, I wrote letters to everyone: myself, my husband, Lukas, and friends who made me angry. I rarely sent them, I just needed to express myself. I always felt better after re-reading them many times. I kept them and reread them until I was ready to throw them out. This can also be very cathartic. Once you've written down your feelings; you can explore them and work towards releasing them.

13. Create new traditions or observations for holidays, birthdays, etc., especially the first year. Give yourself freedom to celebrate/observe the day however you feel would be right for you, even if it means doing nothing. You do not have to do what you have done in the past. Your family may not like it (and even may argue with you about it) but listen to what your inner voice is saying and then do what it says. You'll feel better for it.

14. If you find you are having a difficult time making even the smallest of decisions, this chart can help in the decision-making process. The idea is to do only the things that are in the column marked Makes Me Feel Better.

Task	Makes Me Feel Better	Makes Me Feel Worse

15. Allow yourself to change your mind. Sometimes we cannot anticipate how we will feel once we have agreed to something. You may think you can do it, but as the time gets closer, or you are in the middle of it, you realize you can't. It is okay to walk away.

16. Knowing that a "milestone day" is coming up (i.e.: specific holiday, family gathering, going back to work and seeing your co-workers for the first time) may be difficult. Have a plan for "getting through it." Maybe you could tell a family member how you want to be treated or spoken to or speak with your supervisor ahead of time. If going back to work is scaring you, maybe you could get to work earlier than usual, so you are already at your desk before everyone gets in.
17. Forgive yourself for any decision you made about your pregnancy (No testing? Too much testing?) or the death of your child. Some of these decisions had to be made immediately, and you may not have had the time to think of other options. Unfortunately, they can't be changed now, and you must live with those decisions. You were under tremendous stress to make the decision that you did, and you made the best one at the time. Give yourself some grace, and work on forgiving yourself.
18. If you did not have a funeral for your baby, allow yourself to have a memorial service at any time. If you want to do something more meaningful for your child, examples might include: planting a tree, donating a bench in your baby's name to a park, etc. If your baby was in the NICU, a possibility could be to donate a rocking chair to the NICU, the nursery, or the pediatric floor.
19. Even though you may think you're not making any progress in your "grief journey," look back and see how far you have come. It might seem you are no better than when you first "lost" your baby, but perhaps you can go for longer periods without crying, or without a headache, or you might have a moment where you laughed (and don't feel guilty for that). It is important that you look back every month or so. You will see that you are in the healing process. Remember, you are not leaving your baby behind. You are leaving the anguish of his/her death behind

and working on taking the love you have for him or her with you into the present and the future.

20. Make sure you eat. I know you may not feel like it, but you need to. Believe it or not, it will help you get through the day. Also drink lots of water. Your body knows what you are going through, and it can handle the tremendous pain. Stress can cause physical symptoms/illness so let's not add a medical problem to the tremendous emotional stress you are under.
21. Allow yourself to stay in bed or on the couch if you need to, especially if you are home alone all day. However, if you are in bed day after day after day, not getting out of your pajamas, or taking care of your personal hygiene, it might be time to consult a therapist.
22. Get outside at least once a day. If you are not up to a walk, then stroll to the end of your driveway twice. Getting outside feels good. It doesn't change your situation, but breathing fresh air is healthy.
23. There is no particular way you "should' feel or things you 'should' do. There are no rules about how grieving unfolds.
24. Avoid quick fixes. Resist the urge to drink alcohol, smoke cigarettes, or take nonprescription medicines (such as sleeping aids). When you are under emotional stress, these may only add to your unpleasant feelings and experiences. They may mask your emotions and prevent normal, necessary grieving.
25. Do not make any major decisions during your first year of grief if you can help it. By major decisions, I mean moving, changing jobs, signing contracts, etc. The first year after your baby dies, you see your entire life through the prism of grief, and you may not be thinking clearly. If your baby hadn't died, perhaps you wouldn't be making these life altering decisions.

Unwelcome and Uncomfortable Grief Comments

People want to help, but often the things that they would say were anything but helpful. Here are some of the comments people would share with me, that although well-intentioned, were hurtful or offensive. These should serve as a guide for grieving parents (they are not alone in their frustration with these statements), and for those bystanders who want to know what to say.

I know how you feel! Unless you have had a miscarriage, a stillborn baby, or had a baby die within its first month, you don't know how they feel. Although grief is universal, the grief "feeling" can vary depending on who the deceased is to the mourner. There is a saying (and I don't know where it comes from): *"When you lose your parents, you have lost your past; when you lose your spouse, you have lost your present; when you lose your child, you have lost your future."*

Time Heals All Wounds! Time doesn't take away the acuity of grief or solve your grief. It gives you the "time" to work on it almost every minute of every day. It is through this work that your wounds are "healed," and your grief is lessened. I use the word "healed" lightly, because as a parent of a child that has died, the wounds are never completely healed. No matter how much time has passed, you always know there is a child missing. However, by working through your grief over time, the pain of that searing grief is gone.

It's Time to Move On/Get Over it; he's been dead for a while; aren't you over him yet? Who decides this for you? Only YOU! The only thing we have left is our memory, our love for our child, and what could have been. Some say it because they can't stand to see you sad anymore, or just can't help or support you. You will know when it is time to "move on", because you will take the love you have for your child with you for eternity, but not the pain of the grief of losing him. A tough love suggestion would be to let go and move on from the person who suggested this to you. There is no timeline or magical day for your grief to end.

Have Faith. This is most challenging. Grief has nothing to do with faith or lack of faith. It was not comforting to hear someone say to me, "Just have faith and everything will be all right." Well, for me, the only thing that would have made everything all right was to have Lukas live. Lukas died due to a congenital medical condition. It had nothing to do with whether I had faith or not, and faith had nothing to do with my reaction to his death. Having or not having faith didn't cause him to die or to live. Faith didn't bring him back, so please stop saying that. Some parents go through a religious epiphany or turn their backs on God and religion after their baby dies. Having faith or not doesn't change the fact that your baby died, nor does it make grieving any easier. We may have lived our lives according to the teachings of our religion, attended religious services regularly, and done everything exactly right. We may be good, kind, and loving people, yet this still happened. For some people, their faith is gone. It can also imply that the grieving person is grieving incorrectly, because if they had faith, they wouldn't hurt so much. Please don't say, "Have faith."

Everything Happens for a Reason. Really? This can be very hurtful to hear, and I hated hearing it. Now, I have some different thoughts. If he had lived, I may not have had both of my daughters. I also would not be working with the bereaved, helping families with their grief. It may take a long time to realize that your baby's death was not in vain.

At Least … For me this was the most insulting and dismissive thing anyone could say to me. When I heard those two words start a sentence, I wanted to scream. Because I was suffering, I didn't tell that person to shut up. There was no way to lessen my pain of Lukas dying by saying: *"At least he didn't suffer." "At least he died on the operating table with no pain." "At least you know you can get pregnant." "At least you can have other children." "At least he is in a better place."*

Be Thankful. To me, it was as insulting and dismissive as "At Least." Tell me anything about my son dying I should be thankful for? Yes, be thankful you are young and can have more children. Be thankful I was pregnant with Lukas. I still can't get over how someone would think that losing the most important person in the world is something I should be thankful for. Yes, I am very thankful that I have Jessica and Brenna, but at the expense of Lukas? I am grateful and thank my every breathing minute for Jessica and Brenna, but that doesn't make up for living the rest of my life without Lukas.

How's Your Wife? (To the husband). Many times, the dad is the forgotten mourner. Men have been socialized to be "strong" and told "boys don't cry." Because men go back to work sooner than women (most companies give three days for bereavement leave, while woman can take up to eight weeks for "maternity" leave), many people will assume that the man has "recovered" while the wife hasn't. This is just not true. Well-meaning friends and family will ask the man, "How's your wife doing?", without asking how he is doing. They assume that the dad is doing OK, or they feel strange asking him to reveal his feelings … especially weeks or months after his baby has died.

Swimming Lessons: What to Say or Do to Help the Bereaved Parent

It is very easy to say something hurtful while thinking we are saying and doing the right thing. Please remember, not only is your friend or family member in a very fragile state, they will probably also remember exactly what you said or did for the rest of their lifetime. Again, using my own experiences, I can tell you who supported me unconditionally and who said hurtful things to me. It's been 35+ years, but it seems like it is etched in stone upon my brain. I've listed below some things that I think are helpful.

I'm sorry for your loss (and don't say anything else). This sentence acknowledges the baby they lost and really says it all.

I feel your pain (NOT "I know how you feel"). This tells the griever they are not alone with their grief.

I'm here for you. The easiest thing for people who are uncomfortable with grief is to give condolences and then leave. Because your friend or family member is suffering so much, the natural inclination is to try and fix them. Of course, NOTHING can fix this. I think the most caring and helpful thing to do for your friend is to offer to just be there for them, however long they need you to be.

Offer to do something specific (rather than the usual, let me know if you need anything). That is an empty request, and you will probably never hear back with something to do. The truth is the griever really doesn't know what you can do to help them. They don't have the mental clarity (or energy) to think of something, and then can't call you to make the request. Offer to bring over a casserole. If you are going grocery shopping, call them and ask if there is anything you can get for them. If they have children at home, offer to take them to their extracurricular activities or to car pool. I think you can see what I mean. These small actions will be appreciated by the griever and will help them tremendously.

Ask and really mean, "How Are You?" If your relationship with the griever is a close and authentic one, then the griever will know you are asking for their true answer and not the automatic response of "I'm fine." You both know they aren't, and really listening to what they have to say will help promote their healing. Don't say it unless you truly mean it and be prepared for tears and pain. You don't have to do anything to fix that.

Would you like to talk about your baby? Do you have photos you would like to show me? Tell me about your labor and delivery. How much did he weigh and how long was he? This is the ultimate gift for the griever. You are giving them permission to validate their loss, to open their wounds to you by talking about their baby and their pain. You are showing them you really care about them.

Always refer to the baby by name (if you know it). It lets the parents know that you are acknowledging their child and identifying the baby as a person who has a rightful place in the family.

Acknowledge and include the other children in the family. Even if they are too young to understand exactly what happened, they know something different is going on in the house. Even the youngest child feels the tension and sadness. Children grieve, and their reactions vary according to their age and feelings about a brother and sister. Emphasize that the baby's body stopped working and couldn't be fixed. Tell them that nothing anyone said or did or thought, made the baby die. Please DO NOT say the baby is sleeping or lost. That can be very frightening.

Attend the Funeral/Memorial Service. This shows your support and that you care. If you can't attend, send a letter or note. Many parents will be given a "memory packet" from the hospital, and it can include your acknowledgement as part of the packet.

Remember the Calendar. Remember significant days in the weeks and months to come, such as the baby's due date, the anniversary of his birth or death, Mother's Day or Father's Day. A phone call, visit, card, or text at these times can mean a great deal.

Don't Ignore the Loss. Many people might be afraid to say the wrong thing and open up the parents to more pain, so they choose to say nothing and ignore it. This is such a mistake. Trust me; those parents have not forgotten for one second that their baby died. You ignoring their loss and saying nothing, may make them feel their child has been forgotten or was never important. Again, a simple, "I'm sorry." goes a very long way.

Don't Stop Supporting the Parents After a Few Days or Weeks. Time alone does not heal. Sometimes, anniversaries are the hardest times. Feelings of loss and sadness may resurface unexpectedly, even years later. Parents often find that the first few weeks are full of people visiting and showing support, but as time goes on, people call and visit less, and they become very lonely.

Letters to Lukas

I thought I would share some of the letters that I wrote to Lukas over time. You will see the changes in my grief and understand how cathartic it was for me to use these letters as a method of healing.

November 14, 1980

My darling Lukas:

I miss you so much. I can't believe you are gone. I'm so sorry I killed you by taking those aspirins. Every book I read said not to take any medicines, but it was too late for me. I didn't know I was pregnant with you when I took them, but it is still my fault. I cry all the time because you're not here. I should have protected you better—that's what mothers do, and I failed you so miserably. I'm so sorry; I will carry this guilt with me for the rest of my life. I deserve to.

I've thought of nothing but death since you died ... my own death. The pain of living without you is so big and encompassing, the only way I think I can get out of my pain is to die. Then I would be with you. I don't have any religious knowledge about what the Jewish faith believes about heaven and hell. I hope that when we die, we get to spend the rest of eternity with our loved ones who died before us. So, if I die, I'd like to believe that I'd be with you and get to spend the rest of forever with you, and finally get to be your mom.

Did you know that was what I was thinking? Were you protecting me when I had my terrible car accident last week—where I hydroplaned across six lanes of eastbound and westbound traffic, up and down an embankment, across the divider and into a guardrail overlooking a ravine? Were you the "one" who watched over me and saved me? Were you my guardian angel … making sure I didn't hit another car and was able to walk away from it? Was this your way of telling me you didn't want me to die? I see death as a way out of this terrible pain and suffering. Well if that's the case Lukas, you got it right. After the accident, and probably during my hydroplaning, I realized I didn't want to die. I have to figure out another way to get out of my pain; figure out a way to live the rest of my life without you. How will I do that? Does the pain every really go away?

Oh Lukas, not to have you here with me hurts so much, I can't bear it. I count every single day you are gone by how old you should be. Do you know that sometimes I think I hear you crying? I know that sounds nuts, so I must add "going crazy" to my pain and suffering. How much more can I take?

I was coming back from a job interview on the day of the accident. A job I didn't want, but family suggested it. They told me I "needed to get out," "do something," "get busy." The job seemed liked the answer to them. So, I listened to them. After the accident, I knew I wasn't ready—even in the interview I knew I wasn't ready for the job. I was thinking I should be home taking care of my baby, not sitting here answering some mindless questions about myself and how I could do the job. What I learned is that I need to listen to myself more. Whether I realize it or not, I know what is best for me, not my family members. But, I'm in such a fragile state, I can't argue with anyone about what they say to me or suggest I do. I just need everyone to leave me alone. I don't want a job. I want you!

I don't even know why I am writing to you. Maybe this is my only way of staying close to you; keeping you with me; imagining and hoping you can hear my thoughts—maybe even answer them to yourself. Maybe one day, I too will hear your words and thoughts, and not think I'm going crazy because I am "hearing voices."

I don't know anything anymore about anything, other than I love you and miss you and WANT you. I want to hold you; I want to nurse you; I want to feel your smooth skin on me; and I want to smell that wonderful baby smell. I want to watch you grow up and make me a grandma. I want a whole lifetime together with you. I want the pain to go away.

I don't know if this is a one-time letter or there will be more. I am surprised I can put two thoughts and sentences together, since I have no concentration for anything: tv, music, reading, crossword puzzles, or even following a conversation—whether it is on the phone or in person. I'm so lost. Yet, it is so natural to talk to you. You are my son. and if this is the only way we can be together, then this will be the way we will be together. I will write more often. This will be our "mommy time" … just you and me together now and always. When I put it like that, I can't see me not writing to you.

I love you so much Lukas.

Xoxoxo

Mommy

Mothers' Day 1981

My dearest Lukas:

Mothers' Day is almost over. Daddy is sleeping but I am too wound up. It's been a horrible day. I want you to be with me; to celebrate your birth; to make me a mother. I'm writing to you because that is the only way I can mother you ... through my words and tears. I've already spent lots of tears, so now it is time for the words.

This has been the second worst day of my life. The worst, of course, is the day you died. Daddy and I hardly spoke today. What could we say? I could hardly pick my head up from the pillow, as I had a splitting headache and wished my head could just pop off my shoulders.

No one called us. We were totally left alone. I think someone could have called to say that they know today must be a really tough day for us to get through, or just that they were thinking of us. Perhaps they thought if they said anything, it would cause us much pain! NOT TRUE! I want to be acknowledged. I am a mother! I am your mother, and just because you aren't here does not make me any less of a mother! Maybe the thinking is that being a mother of a dead child doesn't count.

We went down to the shore for lunch. It's a real beautiful Jersey May Day, and the ocean always brings me a sense of calm and serenity. Yet, it was so hard to see all the families together ... having a wonderful time celebrating Mothers and Grandmothers. Will I ever participate in a Mothers' Day celebration with my future children? Today, I can't imagine that.

We didn't come visit you today because. 1) it never brings me comfort or makes me feel closer to you, and 2) we were with you when we held your unveiling last week. Strange how in just seven days, I went from being calm and "happy" about your unveiling, to acute pain of not having you here on Mothers' Day.

I wanted and needed the unveiling because I wanted your life to be validated in a public way, since we didn't have a funeral for you. I wanted to acknowledge your life and your importance in our family, and this seemed the most logical way to do it. My brother and sister-in-law and their kids, plus daddy's parents were there. Everyone has been supportive of your dad and I since you were born and died, and Uncle Marc was with you since your transfer from the hospital in New Jersey to your death in the hospital in Pennsylvania.

I only wanted your immediate family there because these are the people you would have grown up with and been important to you. The service was short, and the rabbi said whatever needed to be said at unveilings and the few things I asked him to say. After the service, everyone came back to our house for lunch to just be together. It felt really nice, and at the end of the day, I somehow felt like I had just passed some sort of milestone. I know I am having many more good days than bad ... not really totally bad days anymore, just bad sections of the day—and not every day. I am back working at a job I enjoy and have slowly come out of my self-induced shell. Only my boss knows about you, as I'm not yet ready to tell our story. I don't think I'm strong enough to tell it without breaking down, and that's fine for now.

I love you so much Lukas, and I miss you so much ... and that will never change. I do think the worst of my pain is behind me except for particular days like today, or other days of significance. I also know that when those times hit me, there is nothing I can do but live through it, experience it, and then let it go. I am starting to think of moving forward and thinking about the future for daddy and me.

When we got home from lunch, there were flowers waiting for me in the vestibule. Daddy, a man of few words when it comes to expressing his emotions, just simply wrote on the card, "Babe, Next Year." He certainly found the right words this time. Will I be in a better place next year, and either be pregnant or have a child? I don't know, but for the first time since you died, I am finally ready to think about it. Know this Lukas, NO future baby will ever replace you. You are your own person and my first-born. No other baby will hold that status. Your place is forever sealed in my heart. I will make room for your brother and sister, when and if they appear, just as if you were also here to greet them. That's what parents do when they have more than one child. Their heart expands to hold them.

I will always remember my first Mothers' Day, and you will always be with me on all my future Mothers' Day. Thank you for making me a mother and making me your mother.

Love and Kisses,

Mommy

March 20, 1984

My darling Lukas:

You have a sister! Jessica Lee. She was born on January 9, and she is so beautiful and lovely. I think my heart will burst every time I look at her. We brought her to meet you when we were coming home from the hospital. It was freezing, but I needed her to be in my arms when we visited you. I needed both of my children to be together, even if she slept through it all.

Uncle Marc says she looks like you, so I can sort of imagine your face too, but with masculine features. So sorry that our time together was so brief, and I was filled with painkillers, that my only memory of you is your black hair and your tiny hand holding onto my finger ... and then you were gone forever. I don't have any photos, so my imagination will have to do.

My pregnancy with Jessica was terrifying, because I was so afraid she would join you in the ground and not come home with me. Her delivery was also tough, and then of course, she stopped breathing, but she's home now ... and that's all that is important to me.

It is important for me to tell you (and I will tell Jessica when she is older) that she is NOT a substitute or replacement baby for you. Each of you are two separate children; each with your own identity and place in the family. She will NEVER live in your shadow.

However, the first week she was home was very tough for me. I was overcome with joy for her and such sadness over missing you. I didn't know why, and it took me such a long time to figure it out. I was regrieving your death. Maybe it was because everything I was doing (like being a mommy), was never done for you. I didn't tell anyone how I was feeling because I thought people would admonish me for not being happy and grateful for Jessica, and also not validate what I was feeling about missing you. Was it normal to feel this way? I didn't know then, and am still not sure now, but I didn't have anyone to ask who had been in my situation, so I sort of just muddled through the best I could ... and this intense feeling of missing you was short lived. I don't know if these feelings will come upon me again. I do know that even with my sadness over you, this is the time that you are with me ... and that brings me comfort.

Jessica is a very good baby so far. She's only almost 8 weeks old, but I think her personality is set. She isn't too fussy, and so far, —no colic. Perhaps the gods knew that after losing you, the miscarriage, the infertility; they knew I needed some calmness and serenity in my life and gave me her.

For the first time in a long time, I think of the words of Carole King that Aretha Franklin sang, that says, "You (She) Makes Me Feel Like a Natural Born Woman." Jessica finally made me feel normal. I finally learned the secrets of the Mothers' Club. I have a living baby to show the world that I am indeed a mom now. You and I know that I've been a mom since September 17, 1980.

So, my precious son, I will end for now. I love you now and for always. Until I have time again to put my thoughts to paper, know that you are in my heart always.

Love and Kisses,

Mommy

April 10, 1986

My dearest Lukas:

You have another sister. Brenna Michelle came into our lives just four months ago, and she is such a cutie; I'm madly in love with her. I stare at her with unbelieving eyes, knowing she is here ... that after all of my pain and suffering, I have two daughters. My pregnancy started off terribly with me bleeding badly, having my first appointment with my OB in the ER—thinking that another miscarriage was coming my way. However, whatever was going on stopped and the rest of this pregnancy was uneventful (until the end when I went into premature labor and she was born after just 35 weeks of pregnancy). However, she was 8 lbs., so I think she was done being cooked! Because she was in such a hurry to be born, I know that will impact the world in some way ... just like you did, and Jessica will.

She is four months old, and already her personality is formed. She wants what she wants when she wants it. She'll only take a pacifier if

I hold her like she was getting fed, so that's done. She has her days and nights mixed up, and I'm really exhausted. She sleeps from about 8 a.m. to 8 p.m., and Jessica sleeps from 8 p.m. to 8 a.m. I'm wondering if Brenna figured out that maybe this is the only way to get my individual attention. I'm told this usually doesn't last more than a month. We are at that point now, so I'm hoping this siege is almost over.

You turned five this past September, and I thought of that milestone a lot as it was approaching. You would no longer be a baby, but a little boy; you would have started kindergarten and gotten on the yellow school bus to take you to school. Your birthday was kind of hard for me because of the 5-year mark. Part of me always thinks, "oh my god, it's been five years and I can't believe it!", but then I know it's true because you aren't here. Even though Jessica is here, and I was pregnant with Brenna. I still found time to be with you. We did go to the cemetery even though it doesn't bring me any comfort. This is my way of introducing Jessica to you. It is important to me for her to know about you. As she gets older, I will give her more information about you, as I will with Brenna. I will tell both of them that your heart was so badly broken it couldn't be fixed, and you died. I will tell it in such a way that it won't be scary to either one of them.

I remember those horrible days in the beginning when everything reminded me that you were dead. We would get congratulatory cards mixed in with sympathy cards and get all these baby coupons in the mail because I guess I was on some list. Well, the other day I got a letter from some photography studio telling me that they heard from my neighbors about my beautiful 5-year old boy, and they were offering me a coupon to come in and have some photos taken. If it weren't so outrageous, it would be funny. Of course, I had to call them up and tell them what I thought of what they did; just because I was on some list from five years ago, doesn't mean the *information is accurate anymore. They were truly shocked and apologized profusely. I hope if other parents got this same letter, they were able to handle it and not have a breakdown about it.*

I still miss you, but I no longer cry about missing you. I've learned to have you in my life without the pain or the tears. When I feel the need, I just talk to you ... whether it is a word or two or full sentences. This is how I parent you and how I keep you in my life. It is really why I don't visit you that much in the cemetery. Your body is there, but your "spirit" or "essence" is within me, and that is what brings me comfort.

As we did with Jessica, we stopped at the cemetery when we brought Brenna home from the hospital. Again, I needed both of my children to be together (Jessica was home with grandma and grandpa). Both Jessica and Brenna will grow up knowing about you and what happened to you. When they are old enough, they will understand that you were the first, and if you had lived, you would be their "big brother." You are part of their family history.

Even with your sisters keeping me busy, I still find time to think about you. I miss you and love you so much, and that hasn't changed ... and will never change. I see other families with boys your age, and I think that you'd be like that ... perhaps wearing similar clothes or behaving like them on the playground. I think that is just human nature. It might make me sad for a few minutes, but then I let it go because I know I can talk to you anytime I want; for those seconds I'm talking to you, you are with me.

I like to think you are around me all of the time. I don't think Jews believe in angels, spirits, or guardian angels but I truly believe you are with me ... maybe still protecting me as I think you did during my car accident. I know that I am a very good mom to your sisters and to you too. Perhaps because you aren't here, I am the mom that

I am. If you are my inner voice helping me to make a decision about the girls, I thank you. I have complete confidence in my mothering. I hope to find that certainty in other areas of my life someday.

So, my sweet son, thank you for this time together. No one knows I write to you. I often think people think that because your sisters are here, I don't think of you. They couldn't be more wrong. My letters to you are my secret, and it is our special time together. I call it "mommy time." Just you and me. I know I will continue to have this individual special mommy time with you. Whether I continue to write you letters, think about you, or just have a quiet conversation with you, you will always be in my life and thoughts.

Love and Kisses,

Mommy

About the Author

Nancy Hovatter is no stranger to grief. Two days after the birth of her beautiful son, Lukas, her precious son died of a congenital heart defect. His death set Nancy up for a lifetime of pursuing knowledge and resources to understand and cope with the grief that she experiences.

Nancy has spent the last 35+ years serving other grieving parents. Due to very few resources or organizations that assisted parents of infant or stillborn death after Lukas died, Nancy often created and led support groups, providing education to grieving parents. Her affiliation with SHARE Infant. Pregnancy Loss, and Pregnant Again fueled her passion to pursue her vocation in grief recovery.

Nancy's heart to serve and strong desire to ease the grief and suffering of parents experiencing the same loss she did, led to her finishing her first book, *Swimming Lessons from Lukas*.

As an authority on bereavement of infant and pregnancy death, Nancy Hovatter is a favorite speaker throughout the grief recovery community. Nancy is a valued resource for her local television and newspaper outlets as a respected authority in the industry.

Nancy doesn't want any parent to suffer alone through a devastating loss like infant or pregnancy death. Please connect at facebook.com/nancy.hovatter or visit http://www.nancyhovatter.com
for resources and tips on navigating loss.

www.ingramcontent.com/pod-product-compliance
Lightning Source LLC
LaVergne TN
LVHW051604070426
835507LV00021B/2768